The Healing Power of Writing

A Norton Professional Book

The Healing Power of Writing

A Therapist's Guide to Using Journaling with Clients

Susan Borkin

W. W. Norton & Company

New York • London

"The W.R.I.T.E. Exercise" is adapted with permission from material published in *When Your Heart Speaks, Take Good Notes*, Cupertino, CA: Center for Personal Growth & Development. Copyright 2000 © Susan Borkin.

The lists of common negative beliefs (page 229) and common positive beliefs (page 232) are adapted from *Eye Movement Desensitization and Reprocessing: Basic Principles, Protocols, and Procedures* (2nd edition), Francine Shapiro. 2001. Copyright Guilford Press. Reprinted with permission of The Guilford Press.

For information about permission to reproduce selections from this book, write to Permissions, W. W. Norton & Company, Inc., 500 Fifth Avenue, New York, NY 10110

For information about special discounts for bulk purchases, please contact W. W. Norton
Special Sales at specialsales@wwnorton.com or 800-233-4830

Manufacturing by Quad Graphics, Fairfield
Book design by Paradigm Graphics
Production manager: Leeann Graham

Library of Congress Cataloging-in-Publication Data

Borkin, Susan.
  The healing power of writing : a therapist's guide to using journaling with clients / Susan Borkin. -- First edition.
      pages cm
"A Norton Professional Book."
Includes bibliographical references and index.
ISBN 978-0-393-70821-9 (hardcover)
1. Creative writing--Therapeutic use. 2. Psychotherapy.   I. Title.
  RC489.W75B66 2014
  616.89'1656--dc23
                              2013031463

ISBN: 978-0-393-70821-9

W. W. Norton & Company, Inc., 500 Fifth Avenue, New York, N.Y. 10110
                    www.wwnorton.com
W. W. Norton & Company Ltd., Castle House, 75/76 Wells Street, London W1T 3QT

1 2 3 4 5 6 7 8 9 0

To Jerry, who is always at the top of my gratitude list.

Contents

PART 3
Journaling Roadblocks and Building Blocks

Acknowledgments

*A*mong the exercises in this book are a variety of gratitude lists. In writing this book I would like to share a list of my own. I acknowledge with thanks:

Margot Silk Forrest, my writer's lifeline, for her ongoing support, coaching, and professional editing skill, and for reminding me to breath.

Norton Professional Books, especially my editor, Deborah Malmud, for being a pleasure to work with, and for her clear, spot-on feedback on my manuscript.

Bill O'Hanlon for his practical, no-nonsense coaching and for his help in connecting me to Norton.

Colleagues and friends Marcia Pugsley, Ann Stevenson, Faye Kimura, Pamela Bjorklund, Patrice Otten, and Linda Teichman for caring check-ins and loving support.

Saybrook University instructors Willson Williams, Linda Riebel, and Carol Barrett, who warmly supported my leave-taking from my doctoral program so I could focus on completing this book.

Hana Matt, Lynn Grodzki, and Ellen Baker, who, whether they know it or not, have provided long-distance support and mentoring.

Jerry Hurwitz, my husband of three decades plus, for his enduring love, support, and patience.

Introduction

*M*y fascination with the healing power of writing had very early beginnings in my life. One day in the spring of 1970 I was sitting under a shady tree on a college campus in Eau Claire, Wisconsin, where I was enrolled as a student. I had scribbled in my journal this phrase: "Writing as therapy???" In a way, this thought was a natural evolution. As an English major and a psychology minor, I have always been drawn to both words and feelings. I had read Anne Frank and started my own diary at age 13 and never stopped. I wrote poetry in the back of my algebra notebook in high school, which may account for my poor grades in math. Words, on the other hand, came easily to me. I studied to become an English teacher and while in training taught from a book called *Transformational Grammar and the Teacher of English* (Thomas, 1966). In that era, "transformational grammar" referred to diagramming sentences to determine parts of speech. The kids hated it. I hated it. My career as an English teacher was short-lived. Later I moved to San Francisco, where I went back to school for a master's degree in psychology. In 1978 I completed my thesis, titled *Journal Writing as Self-Therapy*. Since that time I have written two books, lectured, and taught hundreds of classes and workshops on journal writing.

Fast forward thirty-plus years. Today, the word *transformation* as used in the *Transformational Grammar* book means something entirely different, referring to growth and change of a psychospiritual nature. Even the noun, *journal*, has changed, having morphed into the verb, *journaling*. My almost nonexistent literature review on journal writing in the 1970s has exploded into thousands of books on journaling. Blank journals can be found in almost any bookstore. There are online journaling programs, journaling software, and blogs dedicated to journaling. Live Journal, a social media journaling community, boasts a membership of 60 million accounts. Articles about journaling show up in professional literature, academic journals, and popular periodicals, all touting its virtues. Journaling has become an industry.

ABOUT THIS BOOK

Although you may be familiar with practices such as free-form writing, lists, and even the use of dialogues, little has been written for the therapist about the practical application of these methods for clients. This book is intended to provide such guidelines for you.

You may already be a "journal person," and this book can help you with the direct application of journaling as an adjunct to what you may currently be doing as a therapist.

Part 1, "Journaling and the Clinical Process," provides an overview of therapeutic journaling and the many potential benefits from its use. It will provide concrete and specific steps for introducing journaling to your clients and answers questions about structure and logistics. It will explain in detail how to engage your client in writing a biographical statement that will not only help focus the treatment plan but also provide a vast amount of background information. I also discuss how to integrate journaling so that it supports and augments the therapeutic work that happens during a session. This part also introduces two very beneficial mnemonic devices to help your client focus and organize journaling between sessions.

Part 2, "Presenting Problems and Journaling Solutions," addresses nine different diagnoses and explains specifically how therapeutic journaling can be integrated into the treatment plan of these diagnoses. Specifically, key diagnoses are covered: adjustment disorders, anxiety, depression, grief, low self-esteem, couple and relationship issues, addictions, disordered eating, and post-traumatic stress disorder.

Part 3, "Journaling Roadblocks and Building Blocks," addresses potentially difficult, sticky, or challenging situations regarding journaling, such as possible resistance to therapeutic journaling, privacy issues, safe boundaries, and protection of client material. Importantly, it also reviews those circumstances in which it is best not to use therapeutic journaling or when journaling is contraindicated. Finally, Part 3 also suggests a program for creating your own therapeutic journaling practice.

Throughout the book I have included a number of cases with which to illustrate the concepts of therapeutic journaling. In all examples, names have been changed and composite case studies created for purposes of confidentiality.

I hope that *The Healing Power of Writing* serves as a companion and guide to using journaling with your clients, as well as a handbook for your personal use. Please share your feedback on what worked, what didn't work, and what questions you may have. Let me know how I can help. Visit my website at www.HealingPowerof Writing.com or contact me directly at susan@HealingPowerofWriting .com.

The Healing Power of Writing

PART 1

JOURNALING AND THE
CLINICAL PROCESS

CHAPTER *1*

❧

We Already Know Writing Works

*M*any writers, poets, and certainly journal writers have always intuitively known that writing can heal. What makes this fact important to us as clinicians is that beyond intuition, there is now scientific evidence to support the healing power of writing. James W. Pennebaker is partially responsible for our changed attitudes; his groundbreaking work on writing about previously undisclosed trauma led to the discovery that writing actually does heal.

STUDIES WITH SURPRISING RESULTS

In 1983, Pennebaker worked with graduate student Sandra Beall on several studies to test the psychological benefits of written emotional venting. The assumption was that, like the talking cure, writing down emotions could provide the writing cure.

What surprised the researchers was less the emotional impact of venting and far more the physical effect of venting. They found that those students who wrote in an emotionally expressive and in-depth way about personal traumatic events fared significantly better physically, with fewer visits to the campus health center, than those who simply described the facts of the trauma or wrote about superficial topics. Expressive writing had considerable effects on the body, an unexpected finding.

Pennebaker conducted further studies along these lines. He learned of the work of psychologist Janice K. Kiecolt-Glaser and her husband, Ronald Glaser, an immunologist, who had been experimenting with the theory that highly stressful events adversely affected immune function. These researchers conducted blood tests prior to and after a writing study. An important aspect of the writing was that the study participants were asked not only to write about trauma but to write about trauma that they had never discussed before. The results of this study indicated that changes did occur in the immune system after participants wrote in-depth entries about incidents of previously undisclosed trauma. Pennebaker theorized that inhibiting emotional expression weakened the immune system, and it appeared that expressive writing actually strengthened the immune system (Pennebaker 1997).

Why is this result important? For one thing, the immune system is what protects the body from disease. This biological system is critical to healthy functioning in that it identifies and destroys foreign and unhealthy fungi, bacteria, viruses, and cancer cells. Also, the study identifies writing as a component of a healthy life.

EXPRESSIVE WRITING AND EMOTIONAL HEALTH

Following Pennebaker's initial study, researchers Stephen J. Lepore, Joshua M. Smyth, and their colleagues found evidence that in addition to strengthening the immune system, expressive writing

4

can help regulate emotions, physiological responses, and behaviors. This regulatory ability provides a sense of mastery in managing and tolerating negative emotions. Other studies concluded that expressive writing could affect working memory, stress, and cognitive function (Lepore and Smyth 2002).

Increasingly, researchers uncover new information about the positive correlation between expressive writing and emotional health. Despite the knowledge that journaling is likely to have a positive outcome for clients, I have found few clinicians who actually understand the practical aspects of how to get people to sit down and write. That is partially what this book is about. This book is also about journaling interventions for specific diagnoses, how therapeutic journaling can be integrated into almost any treatment plan, and best practices for guiding clients in the therapeutic use of journaling.

As a psychotherapist, I have used journaling with my clients for more than 30 years to enhance treatment of a wide range of issues, including the aftereffects of traumatic events (either presenting as a relatively minor issue or full-blown post-traumatic stress disorder), depression, low self-esteem, anxiety, grief, and addiction. I have also used therapeutic journaling with psychoeducational issues such as divorce, remarriage, parenting, and stepparenting. I have found therapeutic journaling to be an extremely helpful adjunctive therapy when integrated into an overall treatment plan.

WHAT IS THERAPEUTIC JOURNALING?

What do I mean by "therapeutic journaling"? By definition, therapeutic journaling is any type of writing or related expressive process used for the purposes of psychological healing or growth. It includes writing down one's thoughts and feelings, as well as other less traditional techniques, such as dialoging between parts of the self, mind mapping, keeping a log, and using journaling with eye movement desensitization and reprocessing (EMDR) or cognitive behavioral therapy (CBT), among other methodologies. Clients can use most of the methods mentioned throughout the book on their own, but I recommend they do so while working with a therapist. Integrating journaling as a therapy adjunct makes it a particularly useful tool in enhancing and deepening the work of therapy.

I have found the techniques presented here to be useful in all three phases of therapy. Of course, not every single case can be neatly divided into three distinct phases. In my experience, however, there is generally a beginning or intake phase, in which you get to know your client, gather history, and create a treatment plan or set goals. The second phase of therapy is generally about working with the core issues the client presents and engaging with the client at a deeper level. The third or termination phase focuses on bridging what has been learned in therapy to the client's current lifestyle and providing templates for the future.

Intake: Phase One

At intake and during the beginning of the therapeutic relationship, journaling is an excellent way to gather information about a new client's history. Having your client write a biographical statement at the beginning of treatment can potentially provide you with a great deal of information. It is a useful exercise for the client as well, providing an opportunity to review and reflect on life events. I have provided much more detail on the biographical statement in Chapter 3. Here is a brief example of a biographical statement:

> *I was born about a year after World War II, in the first crop of Baby Boomers. I've always considered my childhood fairly average, but looking back I have begun to wonder more about it. There is so much talk about PTSD and Vietnam vets, that men fighting in earlier wars don't get much attention. It's as if it happened,*

we don't talk about it and move on. But indirectly the
impact is huge. My dad always had a dreamy, distant
way about him. That's not to say he wasn't often loving
and kind at other times, but sometimes I just wonder
what his life would have been like if he hadn't had such
a severe limp from a poorly healed war injury, if there
wasn't another life he would have chosen for himself and
our family.

In addition, personal or confessional-type writing like journaling can unconsciously reveal more than one would expect. By its nature journaling is an intimate sort of writing, able to touch deeply into places that might be difficult to speak about. Especially in the beginning phase of therapy with a client willing to share journaling entries, I find the level of the therapeutic bond frequently increases. Such was the case with Millie.

I met Millie several years ago. She was a mature woman in her seventies, presenting with insomnia and low-level depression. When we met in my office for the first session, her voice was so low, I strained to hear her. Millie responded politely to my questions, smiling nervously on several occasions. I sensed that she was holding back, that there was more to what she was telling me, but that she was unable to express it verbally. For the next session, I asked her to complete a free-form journaling exercise in which she was to write, unedited, for 10 minutes a day about any thoughts or feelings that came up for her.

The following week Millie shyly handed me her assignment as soon as she walked into my office. I took a moment to skim what she had written. I admit I actually wondered to myself, "Is this the same woman I met last week?" Millie's verbal presentation had belied what I learned from her written words. She was articulate, very bright, funny, and extremely insightful about her issues. Had I not asked her to journal, I might never have had an opportunity to connect as deeply with her as I had from her writing.

How the client responds to your request for written input also provides diagnostic feedback. How receptive is the client to journaling assignments? How much time is your client willing to spend journaling outside of sessions? Does your client take initiative or experiment with journaling, or does he or she follow your suggestions to the letter? Is your client willing to write about difficult or challenging topics? Throughout the book, I provide strategies that can be used to help clients overcome their fear of writing and other forms of resistance.

Engagement: Phase Two

During the middle phase of treatment, therapeutic journaling immediately after and between sessions can solidify the work that happens during sessions. Tracking behaviors, noting thoughts and feelings, and exploring significant life events via free-form writing can also be incorporated for deepening therapy.

I asked Randy, an engineer who had recently lost his job, to track the process he was going through. In one of his first journal entries, he recorded: "I'm devastated by getting laid off. What will happen with the house we finally found to buy? This job was supposed to help with the down payment, give Julie a break and hopefully a chance for us to start a family." Two months later he wrote:

> *At first I thought losing my job was the worst thing that could have happened to me. But a lot of surprising other things have happened. Julie got a promotion and loves her new job. I've found part-time consultancy work, something I never thought I would enjoy. Best of all, it has allowed me time to pursue what had always been my impossible dream—to be in business for myself.*

Termination: Phase Three

In the termination phase of treatment, the client's previously written material becomes an invaluable resource to review the work he or she has accomplished. Session summaries and feeling logs can be especially helpful. Journaling may also be used for future pacing or what-if scenarios. That is exactly what happened with Randy. As his work with me came to a close, he was able to use his journal to review the progress he had made. He wrote:

> *I've never given a great deal of thought to why things happen as they do, but this whole experience of losing my job, but finding my passion has been like a reawakening. For the first time I can see clearly what it is I want and not talk myself out of it. I feel as though I have a vision, almost a mission for my life, which is both exciting and possible.*

One of the methods I used with Randy was Penvisioning, a technique I created to help clients capture and clarify goals and visions while at the same time balancing potential stumbling blocks. Through alternating visualization of the best possible outcomes with images of possible difficulties, a more realistic picture is formed, making success more likely. Another exercise that worked for Randy was dialogue, in which he was able to create a written conversation between his creative side and his practical side.

THE BENEFITS OF JOURNALING

There are many advantages and benefits your clients can gain from incorporating journaling into their treatment. Of course there are the physical health benefits of strengthening the immune system. There are also benefits of cognitive processing created when a story is written out, organizing events into a more meaningful narrative. Because journaling is client-driven, it is personally empowering for clients as they take charge of their own treatment. Finally, journaling is simply an efficient use of time and resources. I explain these benefits in a bit more detail.

Confronting and Regulating Emotions

Researchers have found that it takes physical effort to suppress emotions. Conversely, when emotions have been sublimated or inhibited and are confronted in expressive writing, energy becomes available. Immune system function is enhanced by the release of difficult emotions. This means the potential exists for fewer head colds or episodes of stomach flu. It also means that "expressive writing can provide a mastery experience in which people observe themselves tolerating and diminishing fear and other negative emotions" (Lepore, Greenberg, Bruno, and Smyth 2002, p. 111).

Cognitive Processing

Memories that are the result of traumatic or stressful events are stored as fragmented or poorly organized thoughts and images. Because these memories have not been processed, they may appear at random or as an intrusive thought, such as a flashback. After journaling, during which a traumatic experience is written out, fragmented thoughts and images become part of a story, a narrative, smoothing the ragged edges of memory.

Personal Empowerment

Using journaling as an adjunctive therapy helps empower clients by having them become directly responsible for their own healing. Journaling can be a very creative and personally expressive process. With a few simple guidelines—such as writing without editing, writing honestly and authentically—many clients will use the writing process for their own discoveries. The actual direction journaling takes is frequently unknown as the writer begins, but willingness to follow where it leads can provide powerful and surprising new awareness.

Efficient Use of Session Time

Discussion of journaling assignments, such as what the client learned or what insights have been gained from the writing, can be talked about in session. However, another benefit of journaling is that most of the writing takes place outside of the therapy session. A conscientious and motivated client can move the therapy process along by making good use of their journaling time outside of the session.

Path to the Self

By integrating therapeutic journaling into your work with clients, you can provide a powerful adjunct for growth and healing. Natalie Goldberg wrote, "We all have a dream of telling our stories—of realizing what we think, feel, and see before we die. Writing is a path to meet ourselves and become more intimate" (2005, p. xii). The next chapter will help get your clients started on that path.

CHAPTER *2*

Getting Started:
Tools, Logistics, and Structure

*A*s in any new venture, it's a good idea to deal with logistics, tools, and equipment from the beginning. The good news about journaling and getting your clients to journal is that there is very little equipment needed. You won't need biofeedback gear or a light bar. You won't need a sand tray or clay, paint, and scissors for art therapy. As you introduce journaling in your office or clinic, you only need a clipboard, paper, and a pen. As clients develop their own journaling practice, you will be encouraging them to create and find tools that work best for them.

In this chapter I discuss how to introduce the journaling process to your clients and present several scenarios with which to explain its many benefits. I also discuss how to provide gentle structure and support—enough structure to be helpful, but not so much as to get in the way of your client's creative process. I suggest best practices for how to transition from the session to journaling homework, and then how to use journaling homework to bridge to the next session.

INTRODUCING YOUR CLIENTS TO JOURNALING

How do you find out about how your client feels about journaling? You ask! Here are some potential scripts to open such a conversation:

- I was thinking it might be useful to introduce some journaling methods as part of our work together. What experiences have you had with journaling?
- Some of my clients have had success with journaling . . . (Or) Several of my clients had success with journaling . . . (Or) I know a number of people who have had success with journaling.
- I would like to introduce some journaling techniques into our work together. These methods are pretty easy to learn and can have a powerful effect.
- Journaling is another method you could try (like EMDR, hypno-therapy, biofeedback) to deepen and get more from the work you are already doing.

Assessing for Readiness

How you introduce journaling to your clients depends on several different factors. First, you want to assess the client's readiness for incorporating journaling. You will want to know or find out if your client:

- Has had experience with journaling, and if so, whether the experience was positive or negative.
- Has issues or concerns about journaling or writing in general or has had such concerns in the past.
- Has had trauma related to writing or performance in the past.
- Has any physical or medical issues preventing the use of journaling.

- Has a conflict with any other treatment program.
- Believes writing can help them.
- Would be motivated to complete writing assignments.

You will also want to know:

- How your client feels or thinks about journaling or what beliefs they have about writing.
- Whether your client thinks journaling is a good idea.

You may use the following assessment as a take-home questionnaire or simply as guidelines for a conversation to have with your client. If you feel comfortable, I suggest you have a conversation instead of using the questionnaire as an assignment because you are likely to get more information as well as target issues for later work.

Here you will find these points in the form of a direct questionnaire you may use with your clients for assessing readiness for journaling. (A copy of the questionnaire is also available in Appendix B.)

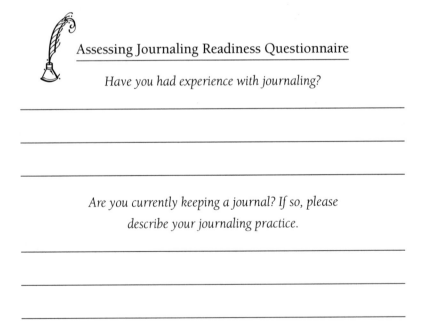

Assessing Journaling Readiness Questionnaire

Have you had experience with journaling?

_____

_____

_____

Are you currently keeping a journal? If so, please
describe your journaling practice.

_____

_____

_____

If you have had experience with journaling, was the
experience positive? Negative? Neutral? Please describe.

_____

_____

_____

Have you ever had issues or concerns about journaling
or writing in general in the past? Please describe.

_____

_____

_____

Have you had trauma related to writing or performance
in the past? Please describe.

_____

_____

_____

What thoughts or feelings do you have about
the usefulness of journaling?

_____

_____

_____

What concerns do have about incorporating
therapeutic journaling into our work together?

_____

_____

_____

Thom's Story: The Case of the Broken Heart

I met Thom at a weekend workshop I taught at a community college. Although this particular workshop focused on practical strategies for writers, it also helped students understand and explore writing blocks from a psychological perspective. In the afternoon of the workshop, I ask students to share a difficult or negative event in their lives that has to do with writing or creativity. Generally I begin with a true story in which I reveal an incident that happened to me more than 20 years ago. I was about to write my first book and had been referred to an agent. In a conversation with the agent that lasted less than 60 seconds, I pitched the book I wanted to write. I was barely done speaking when he said, "It's been done," and hung up. The sad part of the story for me was not the blatant rejection but the five years it took for me to try again.

Thom was quiet. He spoke little during class but had kind, intelligent eyes that didn't miss anything. I was actually surprised when he volunteered the following story. Thom had always liked to read. He had pretty much gone through the classics in his local library before he finished high school. He also read poetry, somewhat rare for a young man who was also a basketball player. When he was a junior in high school he "fell in love." The object of his affection was his French teacher. Thom was a conscientious student. He was always on time to class, completed his homework assignments, and looked for ways to do extra credit work.

One day the class had been given an assignment, which was to write a letter or one-page essay about someone they cared about, using vocabulary words from class. A shy smile crossed his face when Thom heard the assignment given. He immediately knew for whom he would write his poem. He wrote a sweet love letter in French expressing his feelings for his teacher. He spent hours on the project, changing, correcting, and working hard to get just the right images. The following week when Thom received the poem back, he felt like he had been slapped across the face. The teacher had written on his paper in red ink, correcting his grammar, spelling, and sentence structure. In Thom's mind she had entirely missed the point that the letter was written to her. He was overcome with shame. He vowed never to express how he really felt about anything or anyone on paper.

What makes this exercise so powerful is that after I ask students to write down their own stories and share them with the rest of the class if they would like, I ask them to take the paper they wrote on and either ball it up, rip it up, or destroy it in any way they would like and deposit the remains in the wastebasket. The metaphor is immediately obvious and is usually greeted with smiles. I've done the same thing with clients in my office, occasionally going as far as walking outside and burning the piece of paper in the parking lot of my office.

Whether they are students in my classes or clients in my office, almost everyone I have ever worked with has a negative story about writing. Writing is highly personal, and any criticism of our writing at certain times in our lives and in certain situations can have a powerful effect. Be careful and sensitive to events and occurrences that have been traumatic for your client.

SELLING JOURNALING TO YOUR CLIENT

Once you have begun the journaling process with your clients, you will hopefully have no further need to sell it. However, as you introduce journaling for the first time or to someone who is unfamiliar with its virtues, you may need to do somewhat of a sales pitch.

A very effective way of selling journaling to your client is to describe the many benefits. Here are several you might choose to share with your client.

- When you incorporate journaling into your therapy, it saves lots of time we would need to otherwise use in getting history, saving you both time and money.
- When you journal between sessions, you will come to the next session much more focused, knowing what's important and significant, which will help you get more from the session.
- You will find that journaling will help you organize your ideas, thoughts, and feelings.
- Journaling will help you see patterns and blocks, like identifying where your critical voice comes from or how frequently you repeat particular behaviors.

INTEGRATING JOURNALING INTO SESSIONS

You will want to begin introducing journaling early on in the work with a new client, although there really is no wrong time to start. Make it a suggestion, not a demand. Mark Stone comments: "None of my clients journal because I think it is good practice" (Stone, 1998, p. 535). The point is that your client must also think it is good practice. Like any other therapeutic modality you introduce, keep your remarks focused and on point. Use language that is straightforward and nonclinical. Focus on the benefits to your client.

Providing Gentle Structure and Support

Thirty-five years ago, when I began teaching journal writing, I was much more rigid about how to do each particular technique. As I became more experienced, I found that the more flexible I was in teaching and working with a client individually, the more likely it was that students and clients would use the techniques and adjust them to work.

I developed what I refer to as gentle structure. *Gentle structure* means providing guidelines, pointing the client in the right direction, and then getting out of the way. The difficulty most people have when it comes to journal writing is that they are fearful of doing it wrong, which comes from years of being told they were not doing it right. Your client may have grown up in a school where his or her papers were splashed with corrections and swimming in a sea of red ink. One of the most important things you, the therapist, can do to ensure the successful integration of journaling into treatment is to help your client understand that this is simply a modality that has been found to be useful. There is no right or wrong. It might help to understand that journaling is different than any other genre of writing. In fact, journaling is really the opposite of other writing genres, in that the process of writing (and not necessarily the product) is what thera-peutic journaling is all about. Although completed journal entries and exercises can sometimes be useful from a literary perspective (such as writing a memoir or article for publication), for therapeutic purposes, we focus on process. It bears repeating: there is no right or wrong way to do journal writing. Journaling by its nature is a free-form process. You basically can't make a mistake.

JOURNALING GUIDELINES, NOT RULES

That is not to say there are no guidelines when it comes to journaling. The challenge you are most likely to face is how to balance these guidelines while encouraging your clients to use them to become more creative and find out what works best for them. Guidelines are suggestions as to the logistics of journaling, namely, time, place, set-up, and tools.

Time of Day

What time of day is best for journaling? Encourage clients to use this guideline: If you are a morning person, chances are you will do better writing in the morning; conversely, writing at night is likely to produce the best results if you are a night owl. That said, you might on occasion have clients who would benefit most by writing midday (perhaps during their lunch hour) simply because it is quieter and they are less likely to be interrupted. However, for the default choice, I always suggest morning writing—the earlier, the better. For most people this might mean getting up about 15 minutes earlier than usual for at least a few days a week. Be sensitive to clients who have little flexibility as to how they spend their time.

Michelle, Cindy, and Ryan:
The Cases of Morning, Noon, and Night

Cindy was a client I worked with for several weeks before she moved out of the area. We continued with follow-up sessions by phone for for two months after she left. She was a pediatric nurse, working three 12-hour shifts a week. She knew it would be difficult to find either the time or energy to journal before or after her shifts at the hospital. However, on her free days, since she was already accustomed to getting up early, she found getting up at 5 am worked best for her for journaling. On her days off, Cindy delighted in making coffee for herself and then crawling back into bed to write.

Michelle was the mother of seven-year-old twins and the owner of a part-time bookkeeping business she ran out of her home. She was up every morning at 6:15 am; did a load of laundry; made sure her children were dressed, ready for school, and had eaten breakfast; and packed their lunches and readied their backpacks. Once her children had left for school and her husband had left for work, Michelle sat down and did work for her clients until noon. She then made lunch for herself, took a quick nap, and then settled down to write in her journal. That schedule might not work for everyone, but it worked for Michelle.

Ryan, on the other hand, was practically allergic to morning. As a graduate student he barely made it to his 10 am classes. However, he had no problem staying up well past midnight to compose and play music. An artist at heart, he also painted and wrote a column for his campus newsletter. He was most alert at 9 pm. He was far more productive at that hour than during the day. It felt natural to Ryan to gather his thoughts and journal late at night.

Where to Write

Remember when you were a student? You undoubtedly had a favorite place to study, like a carrel in the library, a sturdy old desk, or even the kitchen table. The same is true for journaling. Returning to the same place to study or write helps establish a regular habit, particularly useful on the days when writing may not be your first choice of activities. As different as Cindy, Michelle, and Ryan were from one another in terms of the best time to write, so were their preferred places to journal. Cindy preferred to write in bed. Michelle sat in a favorite overstuffed chair in her den. Ryan frequented a neighborhood 24-hour doughnut shop where he wrote and composed music. Where is the best place to journal? Wherever you are most likely to settle down and write!

Setting Up

Over the years I have learned much from my clients and students about the environment in which they write. Like Ryan, some people consider their local coffee shop "the office." Others are quite particular about what elements support them in their writing environment. Certainly this is not a complete list, but it is a useful start in having a discussion with your client.

- Background music. Complete silence works for some people, whereas others like particular types of music.
- Candle. Scented or unscented candles.
- Aromatherapy. Particularly peppermint, eucalyptus, or other nondrowsy aromas.

- Beverage. Hot or cold, although alcohol is discouraged.
- Rocks, stones, or shells. Can serve as a talisman.
- Framed photograph or quotation. Select a photo or quote that encourages writing.
- Small meaningful objects. Religious symbol or miniature labyrinth.
- Special knickknack or memorabilia.
- Postcard or picture of a favorite place.

Here, There, and Everywhere

Many of my clients travel a fair amount, which at times makes specific journaling rituals challenging. On the other hand, travel affords its own special opportunities for journaling. Many people find they enjoy writing in-flight, particularly if wearing earphones and listening to music that encourages them to write. Some like the diversity of writing in different locations and find it makes journaling a more interesting process. Other tips for travelers include:

- Using the memo paper found in most hotel rooms so it becomes unnecessary to travel with a large journal. On returning home, simply attach the memo pages to the regular journal pages.
- Keep a separate, smaller journal just for traveling. Note the date, time, and place (city, state, country) where you are writing. Even noting the hotel room number can be a reminder of the experience.
- Develop a personal version of shorthand, such as, "Check blue notebook at home for more thoughts on this" or "Find old file at office and compare ideas." The journal writer is the only one who needs to understand what the notes mean.
- Sometimes traveling or changing locations can bring a new perspective. Learn to pay attention to insights as they come up and write things down as you think of them.

Again, there are no right or wrong ways to set a time, place, or space for journal writing. Your clients who journal will need to experiment with what works best for them. Your job is to help guide them through the process if they need help.

Selecting the Best Tools

Encourage your clients to find tools that work well for them. I have considered buying journals in bulk and handing a client a blank one, but I refrain from this. Selecting just the right journal is part of the process. I have found that most people like to pick their own journal. Do a little research to find out what is available locally. An art supply store is another option to consider. For some people, sketchbooks make great journals.

A cautionary note on selecting a journal: it need not take a long time to select a journal. If, for example, a client explains they have not done the suggested journaling exercise because they have not found the perfect journal, you will have more to discuss than how to select a journal! The need to find the perfect tools or just the right word comes up often for those new to journaling. Don't think of this response as getting in the way of the journaling. Rather, consider whether perfectionistic standards are an issue for your client and work with it as a therapeutic issue. Consider the following conversation.

THERAPIST: So how did the journaling exercise we discussed last week work out for you?

CLIENT: Well, I didn't actually do it.

THERAPIST: Not enough time or . . .

CLIENT: I couldn't find the right journal.

THERAPIST: I know finding the right journal is important. I'm wondering what else might have been going on.

CLIENT: What do you mean? I went to at least five stores.

THERAPIST: What I thought about just now was what other things in your life might need to be perfect?

The Pen Is Mightier Than You Think

If you don't do a lot of writing by hand, a pen may not seem very important. Like finding the right journal, finding the right pen is important. Years ago I had a student who came up to me at a break in class and said, "I don't know why, but I'm really having trouble with getting to my journal." I noticed she had an orange pen hanging around her neck. I asked her simply how she felt about the color orange, and she said, "I hate orange." Enough said. Give your clients permission to find tools they will enjoy using. A final cautionary note: There are times when the selection of journaling tools is not about the tools at all, as noted in the conversation described earlier.

When I wrote my master's thesis in 1978, I used a Smith Corona portable typewriter. When I became a serious diarist at age 13, I swore I would never use anything other than a diary and pen to write. With the advent of personal computers, everything has changed. This is another case of no right or wrong way. A professional journalist I worked with once had no desire to use anything other then a paper journal and pen for journaling. She was at a computer all day, and it was a relief to write by hand. I have been using my laptop for 98 percent of my personal journal writing for more than 15 years. For me, it is simply faster and more efficient. Paper journals, laptop computers, journaling software, tablets, smartphone applications—if it works for your client, that's all that matters.

BEST PRACTICES: BRIDGING SESSIONS TO HOMEWORK AND HOMEWORK TO SESSIONS

The transition from a session to journaling homework should be as smooth as possible. The homework should reflect what was discussed, revealed, or resolved in the session. For example, I concluded a session with Bill in which he was able to identify the source of his anger at his brother. I asked him to quickly jot down everything he was feeling angry about. The reason the list should be written quickly is so that unconscious material can surface before it is edited out. Bill wrote down a number of things, such as annoyance at his boss for his recent conduct at a staff meeting, anger at his kids for leaving their bicycles outside, and anger because he did not get the tax refund he had been expecting. He wrote several more things, and then stopped writing, staring at the paper in front of him.

I noticed his expression had changed to one of surprise. "How did my brother get on the list?" he asked himself.

"Tell me about your brother," I prompted.

As if he hadn't heard me, Bill asked again, "My brother? I don't get it. I mean I love him, but we're not that close."

"So, are you angry at your brother?" I asked. Finally Bill looked at me and explained that his brother was a recovering addict, and although they had a superficial relationship, he longed to connect in a deeper way.

"How about talking to your brother now?" I asked.

"What do you mean?" Bill said. I explained how to set up a Gestalt two-chair dialogue, speaking first from his own perspective and then switching chairs and imagining how his brother might respond.

Bill began his dialogue, although he seemed doubtful it would go anywhere. "How do I know what my brother will say?" he asked. This is a common response in both live Gestalt work and written dialogue. I said what I usually say in such cases: "Pretend you are your brother [or whoever the dialogue is with], and I think it will come to you." Bill switched chairs, going back and forth between himself and his brother. When I needed to draw the session to a close, I suggested he continue the dialogue in writing. I explained that all he needed to do was write down the imagined conversation as though it were a screenplay, with he and his brother each speaking in turn.

When Bill returned the following week, he reported that he was surprised by what he had learned from the writing. Frequently a client will jump right in and tell me about or share a portion of what they had written. Bill began, "Man, I was pissed! This thing has been nagging at me for years and I hadn't really been conscious of it." He had written the following:

BILL: I'm glad you are in recovery, really glad for your sake. But what about me? What about the hurt and anger you caused me?

BROTHER: What about it? I did my amends. I made my apology to you.

BILL: That's what you say, but what if I don't feel apologized to? What if I don't feel any better?

BROTHER: Sounds like you might be the one that needs to do some work.

The dialogue Bill had written had not gone the way he had expected. Although he had no greater insight about his relationship with his brother, he realized he did have some work to do. By the end of the session, as we discussed the complexity of recovery, Bill made the following observation: "You know, I always thought my brother would understand how I felt about things. I understand now it doesn't work that way."

Bill recognized his brother might never understand his point of view. However, he still had the option of expressing his own thoughts and feelings and coming to peace with the relationship with his brother. I suggested he might wish to continue his conversation with his brother in the form of a letter to clarify his feelings. The advantage of writing a therapeutic letter is that it is intended only for clarification and need never actually be sent to the recipient.

My purpose here is to illustrate how journaling homework must evolve organically from the session and how the homework is then integrated or bridges to the next session. In the case of Bill, his angry list helped define the direction of the session. As homework, he completed the dialogue he had begun in the session. Therapeutic journaling is intended to work with sessions in much the same way as any homework is designed to further extend and deepen learning. Work with your client to determine what was learned in the session and together create a homework assignment to bring greater depth and understanding to the work completed in the session.

In the next chapter I discuss another recommended best practice—the use of a biographical statement to capture your client's unique background, history, and personal story.

CHAPTER 3

Biographical Statements

*W*hy bother with a biographical statement? The biographical statement is a dual-purpose document designed to save your client time and money and at the same time provide you with a significant amount of personal history and background about your client. In this chapter I discuss the benefits of the biographical statement, formatting and organizing options, client resistance, and alternate methods for gathering personal history.

STEP 1: EXPLAIN THE BENEFITS

When you introduce the biographical statement, you will want to start with the benefits to your client. You might begin with something like this: "I would like you to write a few pages about your personal history for our next session. The reason for doing so is that it will save a lot of session time that would otherwise be spent in getting your history." Or you could explain: "Taking a little time now, at the beginning of our work together, to make some notes about your background can be a real time saver. There are also a number of other benefits, like better understanding the impact your childhood had on your life and how your family influenced the decisions you have made." Furthermore, you could add: "A biographical statement can give you a new perspective about your life story. This type of writing can help you organize your thinking and reflect on the meaning of events in your life."

Benefit 1: Cost-Effective

Having your client write about his or her personal history is simply cost-effective. The more information your client can provide, the less time it will take you in session to do a thorough and complete history.

I scheduled an intake session with Valerie. She was a new client and seemed eager to begin therapy. She told me during our initial phone call that she had two back-to-back business trips over the next few weeks but wanted to set up her initial appointment now, rather than waiting until she was back in town. This presented a perfect opportunity to introduce the biographical statement. Here is a segment from the call:

THERAPIST: I'm delighted you are eager to begin, and I'm wondering how you would feel about doing some homework in preparation for your first session next month?

CLIENT: I won't have a lot of free time when I'm working, but I do have travel time. What do you have in mind?

THERAPIST: I usually ask new clients to do a biographical statement at the beginning of our work together. It's a written piece that includes your family history and major life events. Most people write it in free-form or stream-of-consciousness style. Just jot things down as you think of them.

Benefit 2: Clarification

In the process of writing the biographical statement, your clients will inadvertently begin to clarify events, feelings, and thoughts about themselves. By its nature writing brings balance and clarity to jumbled or disorganized thoughts. Writing a biographical statement is like digging in a garden after the winter thaw. Shovelfuls of earth are turned over, revealing roots and random seeds with the potential to grow.

Fran was somewhat reluctant to begin her biographical statement. Her concern was that she was not a very good writer. I assured her that the type of writing I was suggesting had nothing to do with skill as a writer. Rather, I explained, the process of writing was most important here. Writing, I continued, could potentially help her better understand the events of her life. Furthermore, writing her personal history could provide valuable clues to help her reflect on past incidents, relationships, and patterns to make the best choices going forward.

In spite of my attempts to assure clients of the value of writing the biographical statement (or any type of therapeutic journaling, for that matter), I still often find a great deal of discomfort and fear attached to writing. Be sensitive to this response. Writing is one of those things few people are neutral about. If you get too much pushback, let it go. Use the clinical skills you already know: ask good questions, listen carefully, and take complete notes.

Jake described the process like this: "I'll admit I didn't think this biographical thing was such a great idea. But the more I wrote the more obvious it became to me that I am my father's son, so much like him it's scary. But I also am able to see that I can make changes, and unlike my father I don't need to remain stuck."

Benefit 3: Efficient

In writing the biographical statement, your client will be providing you with a great deal of information, both historical and clinical.

Whereas history taking in session might take a couple of hours, your client's biographical statement can provide much of the same information in minutes. How a client responds to the assignment will provide clinical feedback as well. Did the client complete the assignment, ignore your instructions, put in a great deal of effort, or do nothing at all? No matter what the results, you will have feedback about how your client will approach the work you will be doing together.

STEP 2: SUGGEST FORMATTING OPTIONS

One of the best things about writing a biographical statement is the number of options a client will have. To illustrate my point, I give brief examples of a biographical statement in four different formats.

Option 1: Narrative

For most people, writing in a narrative format is the most comfortable way to discuss background and history. Here is a segment of Ellen's narrative:

I was born in rural Wisconsin in 1959 and grew up on a dairy farm. My parents worked long hours and seldom took any time off. There was always so much to do. While my sisters, brothers, and I always had enough to eat and a comfortable home, we were by no means wealthy. The funny thing was I didn't even know that until I was an adult. My parents both emigrated from Norway and were proud to have become U.S. citizens. I was the middle of five children and at times I felt like one of the "little kids," like when it was time to go to bed, and at other times, when there were extra chores to do, I was suddenly one of the "big kids." I loved my parents, but felt much closer to my mother than my father. My father was a kind man, but tended to keep to himself. My younger sister contracted polio when she was four years old, and it always seemed as any extra time my parents had went into caring for her. Since I was an introvert living in a household of mostly extroverts, I frequently felt as though I was invisible. When I graduated from high school, I knew I wanted to leave the area, go to college, and experience living a very different kind of life.

Most clients who write a biographical statement are likely to write it as a narrative, as Ellen did. It's how we were taught to write, by telling a story starting at the beginning.

Option 2: Bullet Points

When I discussed the biographical statement with James, he liked the idea, but because he was dyslexic, he found it easier to write in bullet points.

- Born 1970 in southern California, San Diego, family lived on naval base.
- We moved every few years, hard to make friends.
- Father was alcoholic, mother addicted to prescription medication.
- One brother, five years older.
- Spent as much time as I could away from the house.
- Mother died when I was 32, cause of death unclear, suicide?
- Father died two years later, supposedly of a heart attack.

Over the years I occasionally have had dyslexic clients, making writing a particularly challenging task. Because James really wanted to be compliant, using bullet points instead of complete sentences was a good solution.

Option 3: Mind Maps

As a journalist, writing was already a big part of Jeannie's professional work. She was interested in exploring new options in her life, so she chose to create a mind map to explore the key points of her background and history (see Figure 3.1).

FIGURE 3.1

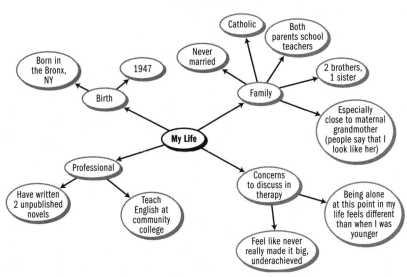

Mind maps are an excellent way to think outside the box and see relationships between concepts. Mind maps use simple graphics to create a balance between logical, sequential thinking and nonlinear, intuitive understanding.

Option 4: Steppingstones

In 1975 depth psychologist Ira Progoff published *At a Journal Workshop*, introducing the intensive journal method, a complete writing program that provides an in-depth life review. One of the techniques he introduced was called Steppingstones, a listing of major life events or significant turning points. Progoff described Steppingstones as "neutral with respect to pleasure or pain, progress or failure" (Progoff, 1975, p. 103). Furthermore, he described Steppingstones as "simply the markings that are significant to use as we reconstruct the movement of our life" (Progoff, 1975, p. 103).

Chloe chose to look at her life experience via Steppingstones:

- I was born . . .
- I started school and loved it . . .
- I moved to Paris with my parents . . .
- I fell in love . . .
- I became serious about my art . . .
- I had a child . . .
- I divorced my husband . . .
- I found my way again . . .

Steppingstones can be written as a list and then each item is described in more detail. The Steppingstones can then be explored in greater depth, providing important details and forming a connection between one Steppingstone and another. For example, Chloe wrote: "I moved to Paris with my parents. It was a time when I finally felt at home, as though I was supposed to be in this place. This city of lights felt like that to me . . . alive with light, color, ideas, and wonder." In another Steppingstone she wrote: "When Henri and I divorced, all that had been light turned dark. I felt like I had fallen down a deep black hole and wondered if I would ever see the sun again." In her next Steppingstone, she continues with the metaphor of darkness and light: "I found my way again, returning to the States. All is not black and white, many more shades of gray than I had ever imagined. This has been a difficult time. I feel older, less starry-eyed, and somehow wiser."

Chloe used Steppingstones to explain several significant changes in her life. Deconstructing time periods in this way allowed her to have a deeper understanding of her feelings, while becoming more aware of her life as a whole.

STEP 3: SUGGEST ORGANIZING OPTIONS

In addition to suggesting formatting options, it is also helpful to clients if you offer ways to organize the biographical statement. Four options are presented here.

Option 1: Chronological

This is generally how most people write a story—from beginning to end or from earliest to most recent memories. For example: "The first real memory I had was of a playroom with a red and blue woven carpet." Or, "I remember when I was four years old and fell asleep in the car. It seemed like we were driving for a long time. When I woke up, I asked my mother if we were home. I remember the smile in her voice, when she said, 'Yes, honey, we're home.' What I didn't know and have just now remembered, is that we had actually arrived at our new home."

Although writing chronologically is the most common way to organize personal history, it is certainly not the only way.

Option 2: Geographic

For clients who moved many times in childhood, organization by geographical moves might proof useful. This might be true, for example if your client had grown up in a military family, where frequent moves to new bases were the norm. I have also heard clients recall memories by remembering a feature or location of a home. For example, Diane described incidents "that happened in the red brick house," or "that happened when we were living in Richards Park."

Option 3: Thematic or Strengths

For some clients, organizing by themes such as success in school, major relationships, birth of children, or career changes is the best way to consider personal history. In his perennially popular book

What Color Is Your Parachute?, Richard Bolles (1970) suggested a similar type of organization for uncovering career strengths. He suggested that readers look at the skill sets of the most successful experiences over their lifetime. In Stephanie's case, most of her successful experiences related to performing.

Stephanie had always loved theater. She had majored in music and drama in college, starred in several productions in community theater, and was in the process of deciding whether to leave her teaching position to accept a part in an off-Broadway musical. It was an important decision for her, involving several changes to her lifestyle. I suggested that she might want to write about the theme of music and theater in her life beginning with her first dance recital as a child.

Stephanie's strength as a performer was not evident at first. Though she knew she had always enjoyed music and theater, she had not thought about them as a career path. Even now she wasn't sure about it. However, after she wrote about the theme of music, dance, and theater in her life, she concluded: "I've never given much thought about my passion for the theater arts. I just always thought of it has a hobby or something I enjoyed. But as I wrote about it, I began to see it as something more. I've been told my whole life I was gifted musically, but it wasn't until I looked at the big picture, of the way music and the theater have always provided meaning for me, that I began to see it as something more."

Option 4: Questions and Answers

You will find that some clients prefer to have the biographical statement structured by using a series of preselected questions. Some people find it easier to answer questions than to start with a blank page. Another way to use the questions and answers option is to provide the questions to simply be used as guidelines or suggestions for what to write. Of course, you can also up make up applicable questions yourself for use with clients. A sampling of questions appears below (for a more complete list, see the Biographical Statement Questionnaire in Appendix B).

- Where and when were you born?
- What do you remember or were you told about your first few years of life?
- If you had three words or brief phrases to describe your mother, what would they be?
- If you had three words or brief phrases to describe your father, what would they be?
- Did you have any serious or unusual medical problems when you were younger?
- Do you remember any particularly difficult or challenging times as you were growing up?
- Please list and describe briefly the 10 to 12 most important things that happened to you in your lifetime.

RESISTANCE TO DOING THE BIOGRAPHICAL STATEMENT

Early on in my career, I learned that for every rule about therapy, there is bound to be an exception. I encourage you to engage your clients in writing a biographical statement, but there will undoubtedly be times when your suggestion to do so will be met with resistance. There are several different reasons for resistance. You may be working with a client who has had some kind of trauma with writing or performance. Some people do not like to write, for a variety of reasons. They may have difficulty writing, don't feel comfortable writing, or become so blocked at the idea of writing that it's simply best to leave well enough alone. The reluctance to write may be part of resistance to therapy in general.

Mark Stone advises that he "merely suggests, illustrates, demonstrates, recommends, and encourages" people to journal. Clearly, he states, any sort of compulsory writing will fail (Stone, 1998, p. 535).

So how do you deal with resistance in this case? For a client who has had some trauma related to writing, you will need to decide whether it would be appropriate to deal with this issue in therapy. For a client who expresses reluctance to the whole idea of writing, consider other ways of gathering personal history. Finally, for those whose reluctance seems more related to resistance to treatment in general, such as several negative responses to your suggestions, it's best to address this issue soon. Consider the following case examples.

I asked Lynn, a 52-year-old bookkeeper, to write a few pages of her personal history at the beginning of our work together. She visibly paled in response. In a quiet voice she asked if there was another way she could share her personal history. I said of course, but I was concerned about her obvious discomfort. She explained:

> When I was 13 years old my mother remarried. My new step-
> father was not exactly the most sensitive guy. He had no children
> of his own and just didn't know how to deal with a teenage girl.
> One day he went into my room to replace a lightbulb on my desk
> lamp. Unfortunately my journal was sitting out on my nightstand.
> It was my bedroom. I keep the door to my room closed. I had no
> idea he would be going in there. A few days later my mother and
> stepfather had some friends over for dinner. My stepfather started
> teasing me about something he read in my journal. He made it
> sound like it was all in good fun, but I was horrified.

Sadly, this is not an isolated case, nor is it uncommon. Parents, other adults, or siblings can purposely or unwittingly cross a delicate boundary when it comes to personal journals. Unless a journal is written with the intention to be shared, it should be considered off-limits.

Larry, a 49-year-old computer engineer, came to see me about issues he was having at work. As my first session with him came to a close and I requested he write his biographical statement, he firmly and clearly said, "No." He continued: "I work with circuit boards and chips. I don't write." He softened. "I'm not trying to be difficult," he explained. "It's just that I'm not comfortable writing and I really don't think it would work." I told him that it wouldn't be a problem, I would ask him about his history in a more traditional way.

Jack, a 57-year-old building contractor, came to see me a few years ago. He sat down heavily in a chair and crossed his arms across his chest. When I asked him how I could help, he began with a litany of complaints. "I'm exhausted," he began. "I feel like I'm chasing my tail in my business, I don't have enough time or money. My wife and I barely talk and we haven't had relations in months. I'm just not happy with anything." He declined my suggestion to do some writing about his family history. When I asked him to verbalize what he remembered most about his childhood, his responses were superficial and curt. Likewise, he declined my suggestion to consider speaking to a psychiatrist about medication, telling me he had taken medication once and that it hadn't worked for him.

I paused. I then asked what he expected might happen in therapy. He responded, "I don't know. I heard you could help me, I guess." I explained that in order to help, I needed to get some input and that I would need him to engage in the work with me. Jack came for one more session and responded similarly. Unfortunately, for whatever reason, sometimes a client chooses not to be helped.

OTHER WAYS TO GATHER PERSONAL HISTORY

In cases when a written biographical statement will not work or is unlikely to work, as in the cases outlined here, alternative measures can be employed. Perhaps obvious is to get personal history in a more traditional way, such as the way you were undoubtedly trained—schedule an intake session and take careful notes. However, you might choose to incorporate some of what has been discussed in this chapter, such as formatting your questions based on geographic moves or Steppingstones. Another option even before the first session is to send clients extensive pre-intake questionnaires requiring only short answers, requesting they be returned prior to the start of therapy.

Some clients who have concerns about writing are more than happy to talk about their history. You can encourage the use of a recording device, such as a digital recorder or speech recognition software. With the advent of smartphones, voice recording is even easier. Recordings can be transcribed by the client and selected portions used in session.

Throughout this chapter I have discussed numerous ways you can help your clients create a biographical statement. Although there is no right or wrong way to do a biographical statement, consider some of the many options reviewed here. Think about Thomas Cirignano's remark: "Each of us is a book waiting to be written, and that book, if written, results in a person explained" (2009, p. 360). Work with your clients to find nonthreatening, effective methods to record personal history. A biographical statement can be a powerful tool for clarification, reflection, and personal insight.

CHAPTER *4*

✺

Keeping Track/ATTENDD

*A*s licensed professionals, we understand the importance and value of keeping up-to-date and accurate charts on each of our clients. Case notes keep us focused and on track with our treatment plan as well as providing a record of a client's progress. Notes allow us to review a case as needed, look back over what has happened with a particular client, and anticipate or plan potential interventions.

If keeping track is so useful for clinicians, wouldn't it also be useful for clients? In this chapter I discuss how clients can benefit by keeping track of their therapeutic work and how you, the therapist, can assist in that process.

"Keeping track" refers to the ways clients can stay connected to their therapeutic work in between sessions via one or more journaling practices. Consider that an average client spends one hour a week in session, versus 167 hours between sessions. Certainly clients continue to process the session after leaving your office. Keeping track allows them to do so in a meaningful way by noting such things as a summary of the session, what was learned in the session, as well as observed feelings, thoughts, and impressions.

TRACKING METHODS

There are a variety of ways in which clients can track both their process and their progress following a session. Among these methods are ATTENDD, free-form writing, simple fill-in-the-blank responses, and dream logs.

ATTENDD

It is not uncommon for a knowledgeable therapist to mention in passing the value of journal writing. However, that's the problem. Journaling is mentioned only in passing. The take-home message is "It might be useful to journal about that," or "Write down your feelings about that incident." But what exactly does that mean? Frustrated with these rather vague instructions, I created the mnemonic device ATTENDD. It is easy to understand, and the double meaning for the client is a reminder about "attending" to what to notice.

When you explain ATTENDD to your clients, you might say something like:

> *To get added benefit following your therapy sessions, you can ATTENDD to what you notice by following a few simple steps. Within as little as a few minutes and sometimes for several hours or days after your session, you may begin to notice slight shifts in perceptions, new thoughts, or ideas. You may also notice changes in your moods and feelings. Try keeping your notes in one place, like a personal journal, a notebook, or a computer file, or you can use a worksheet. The following categories will help you keep track of what you notice.*

Of course, you explain that ATTENDD stands for awareness, tension/physical sensations, thoughts, emotions, intuition, dreams, distractions.

- Awareness: Are you noticing any changes in general since you completed your session? What are you noticing? Do things seem different in any way to you?
- Tension/physical sensations: Are you feeling any tension in your body? Where? Are you noticing any other physical sensations in your body? Where? Can you describe the tensions or sensations in your body?
- Thoughts: Has your thinking changed in any way? How specifically has your thinking changed?
- Emotions: Pay attention to your feelings. Are you feeling relieved, sad, happy, or angry? Do you feel joyous, elated, depressed, or fearful? Do you feel different than you felt before your session? How do you feel different?
- iNtuition: Do you seem to be clearer intuitively? Does your sense of "knowing" things seem different?
- Dreams: Are you noticing your dreams? Note images, people, and objects in your dreams and write them down before you are fully awake.
- Distractions: Are you having any distracting thoughts? Is there a pattern to the distractions?

One afternoon my client Cindy had an especially challenging session. She had come to see me for the first time about a month prior. She presented with low-level depression and anxiety. She reported a series of distressing nightmares that had awoken her from sound sleep. Cindy had suspected early sexual child abuse for some time, but had not fully explored the possibility further. She had heard of false memory syndrome and was terrified of making inaccurate or false accusations. During this particular session, she began to uncover some very difficult memories. Here is how Cindy completed the ATTENDD form (a copy of the ATTENDD form can be found in Appendix B).

Awareness: Are you noticing any changes in general since you completed your session?

> *Yes.*

What are you noticing?

> *Everything seems a little "off" but I can't say how exactly.*

Do things seem different in any way to you?

> *It's hard to explain, but I feel like I'm questioning everything in my life.*

Tension/physical sensations: Are you feeling any tension in your body? Where?

> *I am feeling tremendous tension in my neck and shoulders.*

Are you noticing any other physical sensations in your body? Where?

> *My stomach.* Can you describe the tensions or sensations in your body? *I feel like my stomach is in a huge knot.*

Thoughts: Has your thinking changed in any way?

> *Yes.*

How specifically has your thinking changed?

> *I am very confused and have lots of questions as to what this means.*

Emotions: Pay attention to your feelings. Are you feeling relieved, sad, happy, or angry? Do you feel joyous, elated, depressed, or fearful?

> *I feel most of the above except for happy and joyous.*

Do you feel different than you felt before your session?

> *Definitely, different.*

How do you feel different?

> *I feel both relieved and unbelievably sad.*

iNtuition: Do you seem to be clearer intuitively?

> *I do seem clearer in some way.*

Does your sense of "knowing" things seem different?

> *Maybe that's the biggest change. I've never really trusted my intuition*

because it was just too scary. Now I'm getting that my intuition has been trying to tell me something.

Dreams: Are you noticing your dreams?

Definitely. But I wouldn't call them dreams; they are really more like nightmares.

Note images, people, and objects in your dreams and write them down before you are fully awake.

I did this in my dream log.

Distractions: Are you having any distracting thoughts?

I am having a lot of distracting thoughts.

Is there a pattern to the distractions?

I am frequently distracted throughout the day. It's worse when I have a few minutes to myself.

Free-Form Writing

Free-form writing, sometimes called free writing or stream-of-consciousness writing, is writing in a completely unedited way. When I introduce this technique to a client, I begin with a definition. Free-form writing, I explain, is so called because it is literally free from any form. It is an unedited flow of words written without stopping. There are no limits as to what and how to write; proper grammar, syntax, punctuation, and spelling don't count. If you don't know what to write, I advise, then scribble down, "I don't know what to write." Start with noticing your feelings and your thoughts. Actually, it's not as easy as it sounds. The most difficult part of free-form writing is to move away from the client's natural inclination to try and write perfectly or with a linear narrative.

Janet was a new grandmother, and although she adored her granddaughter, she found herself experiencing intermittent anxiety that began at the child's birth. I asked her to try some free-form writing to see if she could pinpoint the anxiety. Janet wrote:

*I don't know what to write because I'm not quite sure
I know what I'm feeling. I do know I had been so
excited before Kelly was born. It's probably natural, but
I think a new baby in the family just brings up all the
memories of myself as a mother and then of my own
mother. Maybe I wasn't Mother of the Year with my
own kids but I really tried to do things differently than
the way I had been raised. Much of the time I actually
did the opposite of what my mother did. Somehow this
is bringing up all kinds of things I would rather not think
about.*

Janet's anxiety was triggered by the memories of her own abusive
childhood. Although she had kept those memories at bay for many
years, the birth of her grandchild brought the sublimated feelings to
the surface. Janet's entry is a perfect example one of the best things
about free-form writing. The lack of restrictions on the writing
process frequently allows unconscious material to become available.

Short Answer

Another tracking method is a simple short answer form I created for
client use (a copy of this form can be found in Appendix B). It takes
only minutes to complete, summarizes the session, and provides a
chance to reflect on what was accomplished, discussed, and learned,
as well as providing for a bridge to the next session. The specific
components are:

- Summarize today's session.
- What was the most important thing you learned?
- How might this information be of help to you or influence your
  behavior, thinking, or feelings?
- What questions or concerns do you have that you want to
  discuss in your next session?

The simple, straightforward format requires only a few written words for each question. Completed immediately following a session, it captures the essence of what was discussed and helps bridge to the next session. This is a good solution for a client who wants to keep track of therapy sessions and prefers to do only a small amount of writing.

Clark was dealing with issues in his family of origin . Although he had some understanding that his mother's type I diabetes had influenced his childhood, he wasn't exactly sure how it had done so. Here is how Clark completed the keeping track form following a session with me:

- Summarize today's session: *Discussed the impact my mother's illness had on our family.*
- What was the most important thing you learned? *Having a chronically ill parent had more influence then I thought. I think a lot of my fears have come from this.*
- How might this information be of help to you or influence your behavior, thinking, or feelings? *I realize that a lot of my fears were imaginary and I might want to re-think some of the risks I have been avoiding.*
- What questions or concerns do you have that you want to discuss at your next session? *Does this happen in all families where there is a chronically ill parent or child? Was there some way I could have avoided this?*

Dream Log

An excellent way to keep track between sessions is the use of a dream log. Some clients are fairly adept at recording dreams, and others claim they never have any dreams. Generally I make the following suggestions for remembering and recording dreams:

- Create the intention of remembering dreams before you go to sleep.

- If you don't usually remember dreams, say to yourself before going to bed, "I remember my dreams with ease," or something to that effect that is comfortable for you.
- At your bedside keep a tablet of paper, notecards, or a dream journal if you have one.
- Make sure you have a working pen as well.
- Don't convince yourself you will remember your dream and you don't need to write it down. Write it down anyway.
- Write down your dream as soon as you wake up, preferably before getting up and walking around.
- Write down whatever you remember about your dream, even if it doesn't seem to make sense.
- Not every dream will be important; however, because you don't know which dreams will be important at the time, write down whatever you remember.
- Date your dreams and note the time as well. This may help you discover patterns about your dreams.
- If you would like, title your dreams for ease in remembering. For example, the "golden watch," the "red velvet dress," or the "spotted cat" all provide a brief description of a dream.

Because of my background in Gestalt therapy, I encourage clients to approach each significant element of a dream as a projection. Anne presented a very interesting case. Toward the end of her third session with me, she reported that she had been having several dreams about a circus. According to Anne, this was no ordinary circus! In addition to the usual elephants, lions, and tigers, her circus had fish leaping out of the water, books that had arms and legs, and a large paper calendar that turned its own pages. As we had only a few minutes left in the session, I asked Anne to take some time over the next week to describe the significant images from her dream by giving each a voice and speaking in present tense, first-person singular. I also suggested she might attempt a dialogue between the parts.

The following week Anne returned with these notes in her dream journal.

- Leaping fish: I am Anne's leaping fish and I feel like a fish out of water.
- Book with arms and legs: I am Anne's book and I can go wherever I please.
- Calendar that turns its own pages: I'm Anne's calendar and I can make time go fast or slow.
- Ringmaster: I am Anne's circus ringmaster and I am running this show.

Her dialogue went like this:

LEAPING FISH: I can leap high out of the water.

BOOK WITH ARMS AND LEGS: I am different than all other books. I can walk and I go wherever I please.

CALENDAR THAT TURNS ITS OWN PAGES: I'm in charge of time; I can make time go fast or slow.

RINGMASTER: What is going on here? I'm the ringmaster. What are all of you doing here? How did you get into this circus anyway? Are you here to perform? Did Anne invite you?

LEAPING FISH: I am here for Anne. She doesn't know it, but she invited me.

BOOK WITH ARMS AND LEGS: Me too, Anne invited me too.

CALENDAR THAT TURNS ITS OWN PAGES: Anne may not remember, but she invited me, too.

RINGMASTER: Okay, okay. What is it you are trying to say?

BOOK WITH ARMS AND LEGS: I'll start. I think all of us are here to help Anne take some important steps, steps she has been afraid to take for too long. That's why I have shown up as a walking book—to remind Anne she can take all her knowledge with her.

LEAPING FISH: Not that many fish can leap out of the water as far as I
          can. I'm here to remind Anne of how talented she is and
          that if she wants to, she can go far.

CALENDAR THAT TURNS ITS OWN PAGES: Like the book and the fish,
          I am here to let Anne know she is more capable than she
          ever imagined. She is the one in charge of how she wants
          to use her time.

Anne's work represents only a sample of the potential creativity of
dream logs. Stanley Krippner of Saybrook University maintains that
dreams open a magic theater of healing possibilities. "Dream reports,"
said Krippner, "are the only tools available for dream interpretation"
(Krippner, Bogzaran, & de Carvalho, 2002, p. 7). Author and activist
Toni Cade Bambara wrote: "When you dream, you dialogue with
aspects of yourself that normally are not with you in the daytime and
you discover that you know a great deal more than you thought you
did" (as quoted in Chang, 2007, p. 131).

Whether dreams are recorded in a dream journal, in an online
forum, or the back of an envelope, they provide an important link for
clients to stay connected to their therapeutic work between sessions.

CLINICAL BENEFITS

There are many clinical benefits to keeping track. One such benefit
is interval therapy. Interval therapy, so named by Arthur Burton,
refers to the processing and growth that goes on after and between
psychotherapy sessions (Burton, 1965). There is another benefit for
clients who journal between psychotherapy sessions. Personal writing
about the process and progress of the work increases engagement and
commitment to the therapy. Closely related to this benefit is another:
Clients connected to their process by writing about it are more apt to
take ownership of their work. Observing and commenting on your
own progress is empowering.

Interval Therapy

As therapists we know that a client may leave a session confused, upset, or angry. However, the next week the client may have had a breakthrough or epiphany, or at the very least some point of clarity or understanding. Burton describes the process of this shift in an almost poetic way: "During the interval, the unconscious smooths its torn edges, and the ego is also busily at work. The hour is re-experienced, and nuances missed in the crucible become clarified and elaborated" (Burton, 1995, p. 12).

Gina came to see me about challenges she was having in her new marriage. She had married in her mid-thirties after graduate school, began work as an architect, and seemed to be on the fast track for a very successful career. It happened that she fell in love with a man who was several years older than she was, but she knew he was "the one." Her new husband had been married before and brought two children to the marriage. Gina had always liked children, and although she did not have children of her own (and had not intended to), she had gained an instant family. Things went well for the first few months, and then became increasingly difficult. During one particular session, Gina became extremely agitated at her situation. I attempted to intervene with some suggestions, which only worsened her agitation. She left the session angry and upset.

Gina was already a daily journal writer, so it didn't surprise me when she returned the following week and shared a portion of what she had written during the week:

> I've been trying to understand what has had me so upset. I think it's that I had such a clear vision about my future. I hadn't planned to fall in love with Ted, but I know I've been looking for him for a long time. I didn't however, ever plan to live with kids, not my own and certainly not someone else's. It's almost like I've been grieving for my life, as I knew it before getting married.

Writing openly about her feelings and thoughts allowed Gina to process what had come up in the session. Writing into the unknown takes courage. Gina told me that when she began writing she had no idea where the entry would go, yet the journaling produced an important epiphany about loss. Feelings of loss can be confusing anyway, especially so when they show up unexpectedly.

Increased Engagement and Commitment

Randi came in to see me about challenges she had been having with regard to caring for her aging parents. She worked hard all week teaching at a local public school. Most of her weekends were spent visiting with and running errands for her parents. Randi thought this might be okay in the short term but knew it was untenable as a long-term solution. She told me she loved her parents very much but was beginning to resent the burden of caring for them. I asked her if she was willing to do an experiment over the next week. Wanting to feel better and always eager to learn something new, Randi agreed. I suggested to her that she make a line down a sheet of paper or on a page in her journal. On the left side of the page I told her to write the word *guilt*. On the right side of the paper, I told her to write the word *resentment*. I further suggested that during the week Randi notice each time she felt guilty and make a note on the left side of the page and that she write what might be the underlying resentment across the page.

Randi commented to me at the end of the session, "I don't really see what those two things have to do with each other." However, she agreed to do the assignment. When she returned to my office the following week she shared with me what she had learned.

When Randi saw her resentments written out side by side with her feelings of guilt, she realized her thinking had been faulty. She thought, "Of course I can go on vacation; I just have to make arrangements for someone to look in on my parents when I'm gone. I may be the eldest daughter, but I am not totally responsible for my parents.

Guilt	Resentment
Don't spend enough time with parents	Feel like I can never go on vacation
Can never do enough	Resent being eldest daughter and always feeling so responsible
Sometimes I just don't care	Have to be pleasant all the time

I have siblings who can help out. And, who is pleasant all the time? Nobody that I know."

If Randi had not taken the time to explore what was really beneath her guilt, she might never have discovered these solutions. Her level of commitment to making positive change in her life and her willingness to feel the discomfort that frequently accompanies real change enabled her to find practical and workable answers to her dilemma. Randi ended up hiring a part-time caregiver to relieve her and scheduled a vacation. She also enlisted her siblings to be of more help.

Ownership and Empowerment

In my office, I have a small stone with the word *co-active* etched on its surface. The Coach Training Institute (CTI) in San Rafael, California, has coined this word in the coaching industry to reference the collaborative nature of the coaching relationship. CTI describes clients as "naturally creative, resourceful and whole" (Kimsey-House, Kimsey-House, Sandahl, and Whitworth, 2011, p. 3). Although the phrase has its origin in the coaching field, it also applies to many of our therapy clients. I keep the stone as a reminder that I am not *fixing* my clients but working together with them.

Asking clients to participate by tracking in between sessions is a way they can be actively involved and responsible for their own healing. Journaling as part of the therapeutic process helps clients develop a sense of ownership of their therapeutic work. When I ask clients to observe their behavior and then write about their observations following and in between sessions, I am asking them to take ownership of their therapy and the direction of their work.

Lance owned a small business consulting firm. He helped other small business owners clarify their mission and purpose and develop related marketing strategies. Lance was highly skilled at what he did, yet ironically, he frequently lost touch with his own business direction. Although he initially couldn't imagine how it would help, he agreed to dialogue with his business to see if he could get some clarity about direction.

LANCE: I feel ridiculous doing this. It's not exactly something they teach in B-school.

BUSINESS: Yes, that's true, but maybe they should.

LANCE: Come on! What can you tell me that I don't already know?

BUSINESS: Maybe there are one or two things. For example, let's talk about your mission and purpose for a few minutes.

LANCE: Well, I guess I would say my mission is to help small business owners figure out their mission and purpose.

BUSINESS: And?

LANCE: And what?

BUSINESS: So far, so good, but what about the marketing part? Aren't you supposed to help people with the marketing part of their business?

LANCE: Hmmm . . .

BUSINESS: It's just that I'm not clear on our marketing plan.

LANCE: You do have a point there . . .

I suggested Lance write a dialogue with his business as a homework assignment, because as business owners know, it's easy to get distracted by working *in* your business and forgetting to work *on* your business. Lance discovered this for himself in the course of the dialogue he wrote. By writing this dialogue outside of his regular work and after a therapy session, he was able to get a new perspective. Perhaps he could have figured this out in another way or I could have pointed it out to him. However, by trusting that Lance did at some level know what he needed to do, his own written dialogue led him to find his direction.

Michael Tompkins, author of *Using Homework in Psychotherapy*, can attest to the many benefits of keeping track in between psychotherapy sessions. Referring to the traditional description of homework, Tompkins suggests that work done on the part of the client outside of the therapy session offers an opportunity to practice learned skills, generalize strategies for problem solving, gain confidence, and have a better understanding of the root of issues that come up in sessions (Tompkins, 2004). Psychotherapy is a costly investment for clients. By keeping track and completing homework assignments, clients can increase the value of their investment.

CHAPTER *5*

WRITE *to Change Beliefs*

*M*uch of what we do as therapists is work with our clients to change faulty or outmoded belief systems. The challenge is to identify those belief systems that are no longer working or perhaps never worked in the first place. Part of the problem with faulty beliefs, of course, is that they are experienced as true and unchangeable. It can feel as if beliefs are hard-wired, and attempting to change them can prove to be a daunting task, even with all evidence to the contrary.

In this chapter I discuss a five-step process I call by the mnemonic acronym WRITE (what, release, identify, transform, empower). With this tool, you can help your clients determine *what* their current beliefs are, develop the willingness to *release* nonworking beliefs, *identify* the origin of these beliefs, *transform* the beliefs, and *empower* new beliefs. I begin with the case of Tamara.

STEP 1: WHAT ARE YOUR CURRENT BELIEFS?

Begin a list of all the beliefs you currently hold (see the WRITE system in Appendix B for ideas). You need not worry about whether these beliefs are true or false, just write them down.

Tamara was a successful entrepreneur who had worked hard to create her business, chic, environmentally friendly products. She had come from a working-class background and put herself through school, majoring in business. She was a natural when it came to working with employees and keeping her eye on the bottom line of her company. Customers and business associates liked and respected Tamara, but lately she had found herself out of sorts and slightly depressed. What was the problem?

Tamara had a difficult time believing the positive feedback she got from those around her. In her family of origin, she frequently heard her parents talking about what happened to people who were "too successful." She heard them speak negatively about a new neighbor with a fancy car and a family friend who had purchased a new piece of property.

Tamara made enough money to make a significant contribution to her household income. She unconsciously knew she was capable of expanding her company, yet she stopped herself from going to the next level financially. Unfortunately, her situation was not unusual. She was willing to look more closely at the origin of her beliefs about money and success. When I ascertained that her current discomfort was related to her business, I asked her if if she was willing to look more closely at the origin of her beliefs about money and success. But Tamara seemed puzzled. "It's not a matter of beliefs," she said. "This is just the way it is." Even being able to determine current beliefs can be difficult.

Before any shifting or changing of beliefs can occur, the client must have an understanding of what current beliefs are held. Although beliefs form the basis for actions, they are not always easy to identify. There are several ways to approach finding current beliefs. A simple way to do so is sentence completion. Here is an example of several kernel sentences. There are no right or wrong answers.

- Women are . . .
- Men are . . .
- Girls are . . .
- Boys are . . .
- Money is . . .
- Believing in God is . . .
- I am . . .

Another way to identify beliefs is to create a list or a mind map. In a list format, ask your client to write down as many personal beliefs as possible in several different categories, such as relationships, health, finances, spirituality, and work. For example:

- Your family should love you no matter what.
- Once you are married, you are in a committed relationship for life, no matter what.
- Health is completely dependent on your genes.
- If your parents died young, you will die young, too.
- Money doesn't grow on trees.
- The rich get richer and the poor get poorer.
- People who believe in God don't think for themselves.
- Evil-doers will be punished for their sins.
- Work is what you do so you can enjoy your leisure time.
- Right work is the most important thing there is.

At this point there is no need to determine which beliefs are true or false or right or wrong. Just have the client list all the beliefs he or she can think of. I have included a starter list of generic negative beliefs, along with the instructions for all steps in the WRITE process, in Appendix B. Although this starter list can be helpful, it is just that—a starter list. I have had clients respond that *all* of the suggested negative beliefs apply. Clients are likely to need help using the list to identify their own beliefs. Use the list as a guide and work with clients to freely adapt these generic negative beliefs so they explicitly reflect the clients' current beliefs. Remember, these beliefs form the basis for daily actions. Like fish not knowing they live in water because it is all they know, clients may find their beliefs hard to notice because they are the only known reality.

STEP 2: RELEASING NONWORKING BELIEFS

If a belief seems to no longer be working, consider these questions:
- What would my life be like if I no longer believed . . . ?
- How happy would I feel if I no longer believed . . . ?
- What could I accomplish if I no longer believed . . . ?

Using focused free-form writing, write out your answers to the these questions. Write without editing. There is no need to pay attention to syntax, spelling, grammar, or punctuation.

Once beliefs are identified and notably not working, it is easier to release them. This step involves a conversation with your clients about how the belief system they are currently using, although helpful at an earlier time, no longer serves them. Questions such as the following are helpful:

- What would your life be like if you no longer believed . . . ?
- How happy would you feel if you no longer believed . . . ?
- What could you accomplish if you no longer believed . . . ?

As Tamara did some free-form writing on the belief that money was evil, it became clear to her that she had never questioned the truth of this statement. While writing, she began to reason that as a businesswoman she knew a number of people who had achieved great wealth and were very generous in contributing to the community. It was confusing at first to realize this discrepancy in her thinking.

When working with a client's long-term or lifelong beliefs, it is important to have a conversation about how all beliefs, including current nonworking ones, have served a purpose at some one time. For Tamara, as a child, adhering to the beliefs of her family was essential to her survival.

Releasing nonworking beliefs is less about a specific action and more about an attitude adjustment. It is a willingness to see how the belief is inhibitory and let go of what is no longer working. Let your clients come to this awareness themselves. In Tamara's case, she was open to releasing her beliefs about money as she began to realize that her beliefs were not immutable.

STEP 3: IDENTIFYING MEMORIES

Sit quietly for several minutes. Going back in time as far as you can remember, begin a list of all the beliefs you remember hearing from your parents, other family members, friends, teachers, or anyone else who may have influenced your thinking. Add more beliefs as you remember them.

It is likely that your client will need additional assistance with this part of the process. Take your time. This is one of the reasons it is helpful if the client has completed a biographical statement. This process will help bring memories to the surface.

In Tamara's case, she could clearly remember hearing her parents discussing money. She remembered an incident as a young child when she had heard her parents talking about the new owner of a store. It was rumored that the store owner was very wealthy and Tamara heard words like *money* and *evil*. In fact, every time she heard her parents mention money or wealth, it was spoken of with disdain.

As Tamara began to uncover more memories about her parents' beliefs about money she wrote down these memories in session:

- Mr. Smith owned department store and was wealthy—parents didn't trust him.
- Neighbors had a fancy car—parents thought they were "putting on airs."
- Family friends bought property—parents thought they were snobby.

For homework, Tamara continued collecting and writing down memories about her parents' beliefs about money. She could discern a pattern she could now see as an adult but had been unable to understand as a child. She started to realize many of the beliefs her parents had originated from fear and a belief in lack, rather than prosperity.

You might want to try this for yourself. Quickly jot down as many of your own beliefs about money as you can think of. Then try to determine the origin of each of these beliefs.

STEP 4: TRANSFORMING TO NEW BELIEFS

Using your list of current beliefs, select a belief to work with. Now, imagine what belief you would prefer to have instead. Make notes about what it would be like if you adapted your new belief.

Working with or watching a client change or transform a long-held belief system can be a profound experience. Tamara described it like this: "I know it may sound exaggerated, but this is like discovering my parents came from another planet."

Sometimes it is a real struggle to transform long-held beliefs. It might feel like just too much work. You are also likely to get pushback when beliefs come into question. I've heard clients say, "Yes, but I've believed this my whole life," or "Everything I have ever done is based on these beliefs. It's too late to change now."

In the exercise designed to help the transformation to new beliefs, I ask clients to carefully consider what beliefs they would prefer to have, as well as what it might be like to live with a new belief. First, the client creates a list of new and different preferred beliefs. In Tamara's case, a preferred belief might be that money is not evil. Next, the client writes in focused free-form style, about what it would be like to live with the new beliefs.

STEP 5: EMPOWERING NEW BELIEFS

> You have now listed your current beliefs, considered releasing those beliefs that no longer work for you, identified the origin of your beliefs to better understand how you came to have them, and imagined new beliefs. Write in focused free-form style about what it would be like to live with the new belief. Remember, don't edit. There is no need to be considered with syntax, spelling, grammar, or punctuation as you write about this new belief.

Empowering, the final step in this process is about actually integrating new beliefs. Fortunately, Tamara was able to embrace new beliefs, although with some resistance. Recall that when she first came in to see me, she had presented with slight depression and a vague sense of being out of sorts, like something was not quite right, but she didn't know what it was.

When new beliefs become empowered and integrated, energy is restored and beliefs and values are in alignment. This is how it played out with Tamara. She decided to take a week off from work. She spoke with her husband about her plans and arranged with one of her managers to handle any work emergencies. She planned a retreat for herself at a lake resort she hadn't been to in years. While there, she hiked, swam, and spent time alone with himself, something she seldom did. I knew that Tamara had been an intermittent journal writer and had painted sporadically. At my suggestion, she took both a blank journal and a sketchbook, although she told me later that she hadn't planned to use either one.

Tamara remembered the discussion we had had a few weeks prior to her retreat. These questions had remained unanswered, but continued to gnaw at her in a not unpleasant way:

- What would your life be like if you no longer believed . . . ?
- How happy would you feel if you no longer believed . . . ?
- What could you accomplish if you no longer believed . . . ?

When Tamara returned for her next session, she looked relaxed and rested. The vague, out-of-sorts feeling was gone, as was the mild depression. I asked her what had changed for her, and she told me that although being away for several days was helpful, it was certainly more than that. Tamara did some journaling while she was away. She shared some of what she had written:

What would my life be like if I no longer believed that I had gone as far as I could go? I've always had a sort of secret fantasy about what I could really create. Instead of a "successful enough" small manufacturing company, what if my products went nationwide? Or international? What if I really did contribute much more than I had ever let myself imagine?

Tamara expanded her business over the next few years. She chose not to go wider with her market, but to go more deeply within it to create a boutique brand. The important thing here was that she was no longer stuck with beliefs she had outgrown. By releasing the old thoughts and creating new beliefs, she had many more options to choose from. Perhaps the greatest power on Earth is the ability to change your mind.

PART 2

PRESENTING PROBLEMS AND JOURNALING SOLUTIONS

CHAPTER 6

◦⟊◦

Adjustment Disorders and Stress

*I*n Part 1 of this book I introduced journaling into the clinical process, explaining how and why it works. In Part 2, I discuss recommended journaling interventions for specific diagnoses—in other words, presenting problems and journaling solutions. Before I go further, let me remind you that therapeutic journaling is an *adjunct* to psychotherapy. Granted, journaling is an important, useful, and healing adjunct designed to enhance, deepen, and support therapeutic work, but it is not, in and of itself, the same as therapy. Nor is it a suitable substitute for someone who needs therapy. Remember that you are a clinician first, and no amount of knowledge about therapeutic journaling interventions can take the place of your clinical skill, experience, or judgment wisely applied.

I begin this section with a discussion of adjustment disorders—a difficult, but relatively brief, nonpathological response to a stressful event or situation. I look at several journaling tools for treating adjustment disorders: a form of a Quick List called What's Bugging Me, a visualization exercise called Catastrophic to Realistic, a free-form exercise called Uncovering Triggering Events, and a dialogue exercise known as Dialoguing with Your Stressor. In addition, I explain two planning tools: mind storming solutions (using mind maps) and planning and evaluation review technique. These journaling techniques go a long way toward decreasing stress for adjustment disorders of adult life.

James Strain and Matthew Friedman suggest that the core of an adjustment disorder is a specific stressor: "Adjustment disorder (AD) shares with posttraumatic stress disorder (PTSD), and acute stress disorder (ASD) the etiology of a stressful event that has precipitated a clinically significant alteration in cognitions, emotions, and/or behavior" (Strain and Friedman, 2011, p. 818). I agree with this distinction in that I often think of an adjustment disorder as stress relating to a growing pain of adult life. Both positive and negative things happen to adults, such as moving to a new home, a child leaving for college, a divorce, or an auto accident. Yet adapting to each of these things can cause a good deal of stress.

Strain and Friedman (2011) also suggest that the lack of more specific symptoms has made this a useful diagnosis for clinicians. I have found this true in my own practice, in which an adjustment disorder is somewhat of a default diagnosis if more chronic or severe symptoms of depression, anxiety, thought, or mood disorder are not present. Due to the lack of specificity of symptoms, "adjustment disorder" allows for a greater range of presenting issues and hence a wide variety of journaling interventions.

WHAT'S BUGGING ME LIST

Sit quietly for a few moments before you begin writing. Begin to imagine all of the things that are bothering you—big, small, and in between. Without editing, begin writing your list. When the list feels complete to you, review it and notice any patterns in what you have written or if the list provides you with other information.

A 53-year-old woman named Darlene came to see me and told me she had been experiencing low-level depression and periodic post-menopausal angry outbursts. Although her feelings were very real, she was unclear about what was triggering the episodes. It was important to her to know what was setting off these outbursts, and I agreed. I introduced Darlene to Quick Lists and suggested she start with a What's Bugging Me List.

Quick lists represent a category of journaling that can be adapted for many different uses. Lists provide a less formal way of writing that can bypass the hesitation of writing full sentences. As the name implies, Quick Lists are best written quickly and without editing. For Darlene, I suggested a Quick List at the beginning of treatment to try to pinpoint possible underlying issues creating the depression and outbursts. To do so, I asked Darlene to write a What's Bugging Me List. I reminded her to list things as quickly as possible, without editing. She wrote:

What's Bugging Me List:
- My mother-in-law
- The noise
- The mess
- Having people around constantly
- Days getting shorter, dark at 4:30

It may seem as if Darlene's list was somewhat random, but creating this brief list at the beginning of her work helped bring up topics for further exploration. There are times when a client comes in with a very clear sense of the work he or she wants to do. But there are times, such as in Darlene's case, when symptoms are vague and the direction of the work is unclear. Exercises such as a What's Bugging Me List can help clarify the direction for a client's work.

UNCOVERING TRIGGERING EVENTS

> Sit quietly for a few moments before you begin writing. When you are ready, begin writing in free-form style about anything that is bothering or annoying you. Do not edit or pay attention to syntax, spelling, grammar, or punctuation. Just keep writing. If you have written a What's Bugging Me List, it may be helpful to use that for ideas.

I also asked Darlene if she would be willing to write down a brief summary of her sessions, explaining that in addition to her What's Bugging Me List the writing process might be a helpful part of determining the trigger. Uncovering Triggering Events is a free-form exercise that encourages and enables exploration of underlying or unconscious issues. Here are the notes following some of Darlene's sessions:

Session 1: Today was my first therapy session. I talked with the therapist about my family background. It seems like we focused on the impact of Mom's illness. I've never given it much thought. What does this have to do with my current issues?

Session 3: Still not clear about how what happened with my parents, especially Mom, is so important. But I'll hang with it for now. I'm feeling really ambivalent about upcoming holidays.

Session 5: Okay, finally this is all beginning to make some sense. Since I began therapy, I've been doing a lot of reading on bipolar disease. I guess it's not uncommon to be concerned when you have a bipolar parent. It seems like lately every time I'm even a little depressed or especially happy I wonder about it. The last several days with all the kids and in-laws around, it just seemed to make everything more intense.

Session 7: I'm pretty clear now that I am not bipolar. I feel like I have been confusing what I have always called my moodiness with being an emotionally expressive person. I feel things very deeply and at times I've just not felt like that's okay. But it's who I am. Also, finding out I'm very much impacted by the season does help to explain this low-level depression and some of the dark moods I've been having. I think there's even a name for it—seasonal something. I'm also discovering about myself that I'm used to having a lot more time and space alone. As much as I love having the kids home, it's stressful and having my mother-in-law here doesn't help things along. Fortunately things should be calming down soon.

In the short course of her work with me, Darlene was able to identify her moodiness as a part of who she was. She learned that every negative or depressed feeling or every especially happy moment was not indicative of bipolar disease, as she had long feared. She did learn, however that she was susceptible to seasonal affective disorder and more affected by her environment than she had been prior to menopause.

FROM CATASTROPHIC TO REALISTIC

Sit quietly for several minutes being aware of both the potential positive outcome and negative fears about an upcoming event or situation. When you are ready, close your eyes and get a very clear picture of the best possible outcome for your upcoming event or situation. Quickly write down what you see. Close your eyes again, and this time, picture an obstacle to this positive outcome. Picture what could go wrong, what is stopping you, what fears you have, and what is making this so difficult. Now, go back to another picture of the positive outcome and write about that. Finally, find another potential obstacle and describe it. Moving back and forth between potential positive and negative outcomes is called mental contrasting and can move catastrophic thinking to realistic thinking.

Joe, a young man in his mid-twenties, came to see me, presenting with anxiety. He had done well in his undergraduate work and had recently completed law school. He was preparing to take the bar exam. While it is normal to feel anxiety about such an important event, Joe's anxiety was much more extreme. He had been having nightmares, had lost 15 pounds, had gone to the emergency room because he believed he was having a heart attack, and reported that he was unable to sleep for more than a few hours at a time.

After ruling out other anxiety disorders, such as generalized anxiety disorder or post-traumatic stress disorder, I introduced mindfulness breathing so Joe could experience some immediate relief. I then asked him to tell me about his catastrophic expectations. He did so, citing (among other things) humiliation in front of his law school cohorts, his family, and friends. For homework, I suggested that he do some journaling about his catastrophic expectations. I asked him to do some writing about the worst-case scenario he could imagine regarding the bar exam. I added additional steps from a process called *mental contrasting*, garnered from the work of Gabrielle Oettingen and her colleagues. Mental contrasting is contrasting imagined positive fantasies with the reality of negative obstacles. The objective is to use the discrepancy between the positive and negative results to motivate decisive action (Oettingen, Pak, and Schnetter, 2001). In her book *Succeed: How We Can Reach Our Goals*, Heidi Grant Halvorson (2010) describes the steps to this process by beginning with a visualized positive outcome and alternating it with an obstacle.

Penvisioning is a journaling technique I developed several years ago to capture visualized positive outcomes. Incorporating Halvorson's conceptualization, I suggested to Joe that he write in great detail the most positive outcome he could imagine concerning his bar exam. After he wrote down the visualization of the positive outcome, he was then to write in great detail about an obstacle to that scenario. The third and fourth steps of the process were simply to repeat the first two steps. The rationale for beginning with the positive outcome instead of the obstacle is that it is psychologically crucial to create urgency, or what is known as "necessity to act" (Halvorson, 2011, p. 25). The tension between the positive outcome and the obstacle provides motivation to achieve the goal. Halvorson points out, however, that the goal must be something you believe you can actually achieve.

For Joe, it was easiest to imagine the negative obstacles. However, desperation increased his motivation to follow-up with my Penvisioning suggestions. Here is what Joe wrote:

Positive outcome: Celebrating at a big party after I pass my law boards. Our living room is packed with champagne drinking well-wishers. I feel great, proud of myself and excited about my future as a lawyer.

Negative obstacle: Recurring fantasy . . . I go blank. Everything around me is dark. There is no light any-where. Everything I ever knew about the law has fallen out of my brain, never to be retrieved again.

Positive outcome: I am proudly hanging my newly framed certification on the wall of my office. I am about to see my first client in what turns out to be a very suc-cessful settlement.

Negative obstacle: Every time I sit down to study, the words blur and I have a picture in my mind of my entire law school class jeering and pointing at me because I have failed to pass the bar exam.

From Catastrophic to Realistic helped Joe in a number of ways. By repeating this exercise for several days in a row, he was able to break out of his negative thinking cycle. He also became aware that while his positive outcome visions were fantasies, his negative obstacles were fantasies as well. Eventually Joe reached a greater sense of balance, a kind of realistic optimism, by pairing negative fears with positive outcomes.

DIALOGUING WITH YOUR STRESSOR

Identify the core of the stressor; what is causing the stress? Create a dialogue between the stressor and the part of you wanting to resolve the stress. Name both aspects of the dialogue. Write the dialogue as though it was a screenplay, both sides taking turns speaking. Continue with the dialogue until a resolution is reached.

Haley came in to see me about a situation she was struggling with. As she sat down she explained, "I feel ridiculous even being here. I mean this is such a great opportunity for me and yet I feel really confused and upset. What's wrong with me?"

As she explained her situation further, it became obvious that nothing was wrong with her; she was having difficulty adjusting to a new challenge. She had just been notified of an opportunity to study abroad for a minimum of a year, and although it was something she had always wanted to do, she was in the middle of several important projects at her current job, she was completing a remodel of her home, and her close friend had just been in a serious accident. "I don't know what to do," she said. "There's just too much going on."

I asked Haley if she would consider talking with what was making her feel so stressed out. She looked at me oddly and said, "Excuse me?" I repeated what I had just said and added, "It seems to me that your struggle is internal. One part of you is thrilled at the opportunity you have, while the other part of you is struggling with all the reasons you shouldn't go."

"I guess that's true," she responded, as though she didn't quite believe it was so. I suggested Haley try an experiment. I asked her to use two chairs in my office. One chair would represent the part of her that wanted to take advantage of the opportunity she had to study abroad. The other chair would represent the reasons she should not. She reluctantly agreed to my suggestion. I asked which part was feeling the strongest at that moment. She said it was all the reasons she shouldn't go. This is how the dialogue began:

THIS IS NOT A GOOD IDEA: I can't leave now! I'm in the middle of
a bunch of projects, I'm in the middle of a remodel,
and my dear friend will need me to be here during her
recovery.

OMG! WHAT A GREAT OPPORTUNITY: Yes but, you have been wanting
this chance practically your whole life.

THIS IS NOT A GOOD IDEA: The timing on this just sucks.

OMG! WHAT A GREAT OPPORTUNITY: Maybe so. But here's the thing—
you have a very full life. Will there ever be a good time?

It became clear to both of us that Haley understood the dialogue concept and would be able to complete the dialogue on her own in writing outside of the session. Here is part of what she wrote:

THIS IS NOT A GOOD IDEA: I could find out if I could postpone the
start date.

OMG! WHAT A GREAT OPPORTUNITY: You absolutely could do that,
but you could also consider these ideas: Can you get
someone to take over the management of your projects?
Can you get someone to oversee the remodeling of your
house? What if you were able to check in with your
friend by email, phone, or Skype every day?

In her written dialogue Haley continued to debate the merits of taking the opportunity presented to her and the reasons she should not take the opportunity at this time. Eventually through her writing, she did decide to go.

I have been using this method for more than 40 years in my personal journal and have consistently found it to be one of the most creative and beneficial of any journaling techniques. My own work with written dialogues evolved from many years as a client and student of Gestalt therapy, essentially creating gestalt-type dialogues in written form. I return to dialogues numerous times throughout the book.

There are some additional points I want to make about the use of the dialogue. First, by having the client start the dialogue in my office, I can see whether the concept is understood. When it becomes clear the client knows how the dialogue process works, no longer needing prompts from me, it can become a homework assignment.

The names given to the two parts of the dialogue can be very simple, like "The Good Side" and "The Bad Side," but I like to encourage clients to name the parts more creatively, distilling their essences.

MIND STORMING SOLUTIONS

Begin with a key concern or topic in the middle of a piece of paper. Put a circle around the concern or topic. This is your main idea. Draw lines and additional circles to attach subpoints or solutions to the main idea.

Ally, a 38-year-old woman employed as a designer in a large software company, came to see me when she began having trouble at work. She had recently received a review from her supervisor that was less than stellar. She had also been having some interpersonal difficulties with members of her team. When Ally described her work situation in some detail it became clear to me that she was a capable and talented woman but had begun to feel creatively stifled. Unfortunately, her relationships with her coworkers had suffered because of it. Ally knew she had to make some changes in her professional life, but she had no idea where to begin.

I suggested that she might want to experiment with a type of brainstorming that incorporated the use of mind maps, what I call Mind Storming Solutions. Although she was somewhat familiar with mind maps, I gave Ally a brief explanation. She was to write a key concern in the middle of a piece of paper and circle it. As she brainstormed solutions, she would attach lines linking the solutions to the key concern.

Ally came up with the diagram shown in Figure 6.1 on the following page.

Ally and I talked about what she had done so far. Although she found the exercise useful, she seemed slightly disappointed, as though nothing had or would really change. As we talked further it seemed to me that something was missing. All of her ideas were interesting; many were quite practical—too practical.

FIGURE 6.1

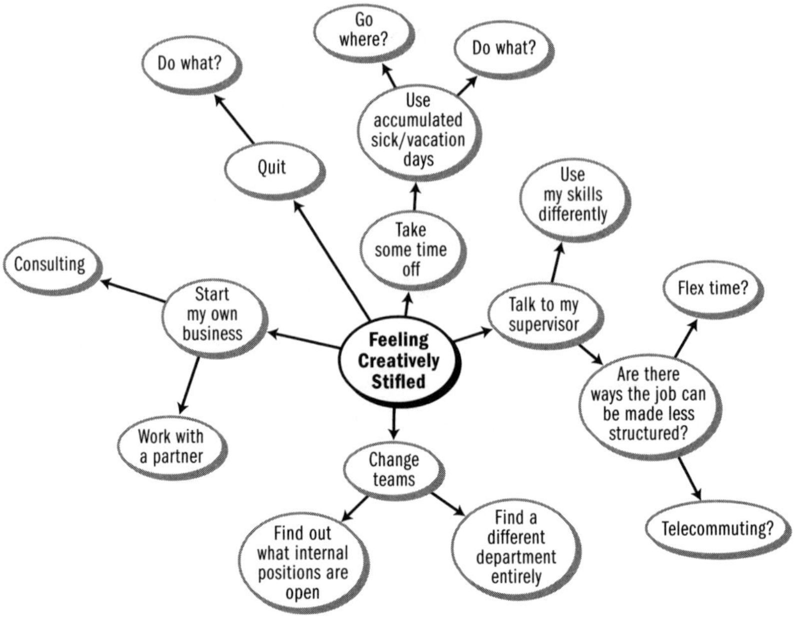

I asked Ally if she would be willing to do one more thing. I suggested she create a new mind map. I told her to not edit at all, but to really let herself get as creative as possible.

"You mean I should get wild and crazy?" she asked.

"Absolutely, " I replied. "And," I suggested, "if you don't like the circles, use squares, or triangles. You could even use a tree. It doesn't matter. A mind map is just a place to play and store ideas." Ally looked thoughtful as she left the session. When she returned the next week, she was grinning. Like an excited child she showed me her mind map (see Figure 6.2)

It was easy to see why she was so excited. Ally had gone beyond what was merely interesting and practical in her second mind map attempt. When Ally she created her tree mind map she needed to do

FIGURE 6.2

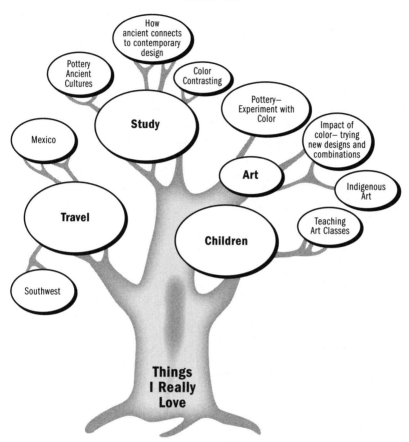

some thinking about what she truly loved and was most passionate about. Ally knew she had always been drawn to travel, learning, art, and almost anything to do with children. The tree-style mind map she had drawn represented the larger branches of her various interests. The smaller branches represented her interests in more detail.

When Ally came in to see me she originally presented with work difficulties. I see this frequently: individuals trapped in a well-paying job but not doing well-loved work. Fortunately, Ally was able to understand that what she loved and what she was currently doing were completely different.

Mind maps are a great device for getting perspective. As Ally and I spoke further, she began to understand that the career path she had chosen had to do with what other people wanted for her. She had listened carefully to her parents and followed a career path that would allow her financial stability. However, when she compared the idea of staying where she was versus doing the work she loved, she knew she had to make some changes. Ally knew it would be unrealistic and impractical for her to simply quit her job and walk out. Being able to have a clear sense of where she was and where she wanted to go was important to her in being able to transition into a new direction. However, she felt stuck and had no idea where to begin and how to plan.

PERT

Beginning with the final task to complete a project, work backwards until you get to the first step. You may put each step in a list, or inside a circle or square. To begin your project, reverse the order of the steps and get started.

In the 1950s, the U.S. Navy began using a technique called PERT, or Program Evaluation and Review Technique, which was used for project management. In the 1970s, I learned a similar and related type of PERT called Planning and Evaluation Review Technique. What makes this planning tool different from simply creating a task list is that, like the mind map, it allows one to see perspective and relationship to other aspects of a project.

It occurred to me that because Ally had responded so favorably to the use of the mind map, she might also find a PERT chart useful. In a PERT chart, not unlike Stephen Covey's second habit of highly effective people, "begin with the end in mind" (Covey, 1989, p. 95). For example, taking one goal at a time, Ally chose to begin with bringing more art into her life. I suggested Ally go to the bottom of the page of a large sketchpad and write down what completion of that goal would look like. After thinking about it for a few minutes, she said she wanted to be doing more art, especially pottery, and experimenting with new glazes she had recently seen in a magazine. Ally explained that she had a room in her house off the garage that she was currently using for storage, but she had always intended to have an art studio in her home. She described the scene: "I am working in my former storage room, which I have converted into an art studio. Sunlight is streaming in through the window and I am happily glazing a pot, experimenting with a new glaze."

I asked her to summarize the scene in a few words and write that down on the bottom right corner of the page. Ally wrote: "Working happily in studio." Then I asked her what the step before working in her studio would look like. "I would need to have the studio," she said with a laugh. "That's true," I said, "but to create the working happily in studio scene, what is the one step before that?"

Ally replied, "The studio would need to be complete with equipment and supplies," she said, catching on quickly. I asked her to write that down in just a few words, next to "working happily in studio." She wrote: "Completed art studio." Ally continued working through the steps so that starting from the lower right corner she had all the tasks she would need to do written out in reverse order (see Figure 6.3).

FIGURE 6.3

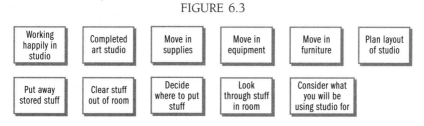

Ally saw the next step coming before I even explained it. "I know," she said, "Reverse the order and I will have the steps going the right way." I explained that not only could the steps be put in order but because she had written them with the end in mind, she was less likely to miss steps or have something important fall through the cracks.

Here is what Ally came up with:

1. Consider what you will be using studio for
2. Look through stuff in room
3. Decide where to put stored stuff
4. Clear stuff out of room
5. Put away stored stuff
6. Plan layout of studio
7. Move in furniture
8. Move in equipment
9. Move in supplies
10. Completed art studio
11. Working happily in studio

By creating a PERT chart, Ally was able to do actual planning of discrete tasks. All she needed to do was put dates and add a timeline to the project before she got started creating and working in her art studio.

Adjustment disorders will likely always be a part of the life of anyone who chooses to grow and change. But no matter how difficult these struggles may be, they are temporary. The therapeutic journaling exercises suggested here can be a helpful adjunct to working through these short-term challenges.

CHAPTER 7

Anxiety Disorders

*S*ome years ago, cognitive behavioral therapy became a top treatment of choice for anxiety, partly due to the fact that the psychotherapy field was entering a new era of short-term therapy. Managed health care was particularly responsive to this methodology because of the emphasis on fewer sessions. In this chapter I introduce a type of cognitive behavioral therapy based on the work of Albert Ellis. In addition I introduce journaling exercises to be used for a diagnosis of anxiety, including generalized anxiety disorder, panic disorder, and social anxiety. These exercises include the Worry List, the Worry Log, Health Tracking, Nature Walk and Write, and Fantasy Island.

Cognitive behavioral therapy is something of an umbrella term that encompasses a number of related types of therapy including rational emotive behavior therapy, cognitive therapy, rational behavior therapy, rational living therapy, schema focused therapy, and dialectical behavior therapy (National Association of Cognitive-Behavioral Therapists, 2013).

Historically the first cognitive type of psychotherapy, rational emotive therapy, was introduced by Albert Ellis in the mid-1950s. It was later revised by Ellis and called rational emotive behavior therapy. Other important contributors to the development of cognitive therapy were Aaron Beck, David Burns, and Marsha Linehan. For my purposes here, I focus on Ellis's ABCDE model because it is relatively easy for clients to work with.

ABCDE MODEL

In writing, describe the activating event or situation that has caused your discomfort. Write down the beliefs you have because of this event or situation. Now write down the consequences of having those beliefs. Working with each belief in turn, write as many disputations to that belief as possible. Be creative! Now write down your effective new beliefs.

The ABCDE approach is a cognitive model that broadens perspective on how events or situations are understood. It is based on the notion that much of anxiety is caused by incorrect or erroneous understanding of events. This approach challenges the inaccurate beliefs through the use of disputation. In Ellis's model the letters ABCDE stand for activating event, beliefs about event, consequences of the belief, disputation of the belief, and effective new belief.

Jim, a 46-year-old man with a history of anxiety, had just completed a series of interviews for a new position. When he came in to see me, he reported that he had not gotten the position and was clearly agitated and upset. I introduced the ABCDE method of cognitive therapy in the following way. First, I asked him to consider the event that had caused his anxiety. Although it was rather obvious why Jim was upset, identifying the activating event allowed him to focus on the fact that something had happened to create his current upset. Of course he responded that the activating event had been not getting the position he had interviewed for.

I next asked what he now believed about that event. "What's to believe?" he asked. "I didn't get the job and clearly I'm screwed."

"I'm not so sure," I replied. I asked again, "What do you believe about yourself based on not getting the job?"

Jim replied, "Like I said, I'm screwed."

I handed him a tablet of paper and said, "So write down 'I'm screwed.'" I waited a moment for Jim to finish writing. "What else? What other things do you believe to be true?"

"I'm lousy at interviewing."

I pointed to the paper and Jim wrote down "I'm lousy at interviewing." "What else?" I asked. He now appeared to warm to the task. He wrote down in quick succession: "I blew it and I'll never get a job." "Those guys had no intention of hiring me in the first place." "Obviously, I don't know what I'm doing."

"Based on these beliefs, what's going to happen?" I asked. I saw a brief moment of understanding cross his face.

He replied slowly, "This is going to be one heck of a difficult job search."

I suggested he make a note of that under consequences. "What are some additional consequences of these beliefs?"

Making notes and speaking at the same time Jim said, "I feel like crap about myself, and that's sure not going to help me find a job."

"Now, we are going to dispute these 'facts,'" I said, putting imaginary quotes around the word *facts*.

When he looked puzzled I said, "I'll help with first one. How do you know you're screwed? And what makes you sure you're lousy at interviewing? Maybe you had lousy interviewers."

Jim gave me a small grin, catching on. "Yeah, and I don't know if I'll never get a job." He took a minute and began scribbling rapidly, adding to his list of disputations. He wrote: "I have no idea whether or not they had any intention of hiring me." "I do know what I'm doing; this interview just didn't work out."

Jim never completed the final portion of the model, effective new belief. He didn't need to; he already knew the effect his new beliefs had. The ABCDE model of cognitive therapy is clearly useful for changing anxiety-producing beliefs. The added benefit of writing down each steps is that it helps track the process and make it more visible, hence easier to understand.

Beliefs and disputations may be written in the following way:

Belief	Disputation
I didn't get the job and clearly I'm screwed	Maybe it wasn't such a great company

Alternatively, the belief may be written in a list format with the disputation following, like this:

- Belief: I didn't get the job and clearly I'm screwed.
- Disputation: Maybe it wasn't such a great company.

A sample Reducing Anxiety: ABCDE worksheet can be found in Appendix B.

WORRY LIST

Become quiet. Take a few minutes to consider everything that has been bothering or worrying you. Begin a list titled "I am worried about"; jot down everything you can think of. There is no need to hurry through this list. Take your time. You may add to the list at any time. If the word "worry" doesn't fit for you, try using another word instead.

It's easy to overlook lists because they are so simple. However, this format for a Quick List can be very powerful. A Worry List for clients presenting with anxiety is a list in which the client is to quickly write down everything that is currently worrying him or her. Here is how I used a Worry List with Christie.

Christie was a 39-year-old-woman, a wife, and mother of two. I had met her years ago, but there had been a lengthy break since I had last seen her. She presented with moderate sleep disturbance and low-level anxiety. After getting a brief history and skimming again through her biographical statement, I suggested she visit her primary care physician to rule out medical causes, such as sleep apnea or restless legs syndrome. No medical condition was present.

Christie and I discussed her upcoming birthday and the fact that significant birthdays sometimes have more of an emotional impact than one might expect, especially for years ending in zero. Next we discussed what literally keeps the client up at night. "Oh, you know," she replied, "Pretty much everything." I smiled and asked her if she can be more specific. "Living in the city, constantly having to look over my shoulder, the boys not being able to play outside or take the bus, double-checking to make sure nothing is visible through a car window."

I suggested that every night, about a half hour before bed, Christie write a Worry List of everything that was worrying or bothering her. No matter how insignificant the concern may seem, she was to write it down. I suggested that the simple act of writing down each worry or concern, particularly prior to sleep, could help ease the constant repetitive thought pattern.

The next session Christie shared her Worry List with me. She had written about what we had already discussed and had added several more concerns:

I Worry About
- Living in the city
- Whether it's a safe place to raise the boys

- How careful I need to be, constantly vigilant
- Going to family "reunion"
- Seeing my brother again
- Turning 40
- Not feeling useful
- Feeling I wasted my education

From this list, you might have noticed there are three different types of worry. There is worry about what is happening at present (living in the city), anticipatory worry (seeing my brother again), and what has happened in the past (feeling I wasted my education). By definition, generalized anxiety disorder means worry is present on a constant basis. The bottom line with anxiety is that it doesn't go away, but it can be managed. In a Worry List, noting and acknowledging worry is a form of managing it.

WORRY LOG

> On a piece of paper or on a spreadsheet, create five columns with these headings: Date, Time, Thought, Physical, and Emotional. Each time you become aware of worry, note the date, time, thought, physical sensation, and emotional reaction. Bring your log with you to your sessions to become more aware and better understand your worry patterns.

The Worry List was somewhat helpful particularly with her sleep disturbance, but Christie soon reported that she was still feeling some anxiety. She told me she couldn't really identify or where the anxiety was coming from or what it was about, just that it seemed to come out of the blue. I asked if she would be willing to track the incidents of anxiety as they occurred for a week or so. On a tablet of paper, I quickly sketched out five columns and then added five headings.

Date	Time	Thought	Physical	Emotional

I was asking Christie to note details each time she had a thought that made her feel anxious. I suggested she create a simple spreadsheet or carry a small notebook around with her. The following week she returned, telling me that she hadn't gotten down every instance of anxiety, but she had managed to record most of the incidents. She showed me part of what she had written:

Date	Time	Thought	Physical	Emotional
3/6	Afternoon	Seeing my family	Tension—neck	Worry
3/6	6:00 pm	Should we be eating better?	Feel bloated, fat	Depressed
3/7	9:00 am	Skip Zumba class?	Lazy, tired	Blah
3/7	1:00 pm	What will it be like with my brother?	Stomach upset	Tense
3/7	9:30 pm	What should I tell mom?	Stomach upset	On edge
3/8	8:30 am	Not liking this	—	Cranky

Christie said that although writing down her thoughts, physical sensations, and emotions was "not that much fun," she had come up with what she thought might be making her anxious. "I think there are two things," she said. "I don't know if they are related or not." I suggested we take them one at a time.

"I'm not really doing anything all that important. I mean I'm a mom, I work out, I volunteer at school, I drive the carpool. But what does it all mean?" I recalled the discussion we had had a few weeks prior about Christie's upcoming birthday, now only a week away. As we talked further, it became clear to me that turning 40 was going to be a bigger issue than Christie had anticipated. It wasn't just getting older that was concerning her, but more about where she felt she should be in life and whether what she was currently doing was making her happy.

The second big area of concern was a family reunion coming up in early summer. When I had first worked with Christie some years ago, she had done a great deal of good work on getting over molestation by her brother when she was a child. She had not yet confronted her family in person and was anxious about what it would be like.

Christie continued in therapy for several weeks, dealing with how she would deal with her family on seeing them again and the issue of whether she wanted to return to the workforce and pursue her aborted career in law. As it happened, she managed the confrontation with her family fairly well, although it was difficult and quite uncomfortable for her. She also decided to go back into the workforce and became a full-time working mom. It is likely that eventually Christie would have been able to pinpoint these concerns, but I believe her Worry List and Worry Log were useful tools in helping her understand her anxiety and do what was necessary to dissipate it.

As in the Worry List, the Worry Log is about managing symptoms. The Worry Log helps identify triggers, making management of anxiety easier. For example, when your client brings in a Worry Log, you can work together to spot patterns and prepare strategies to cope with anxiety.

HEALTH TRACKING

On a sheet of paper or on a spreadsheet, create as many columns as necessary to record the areas you are interested in tracking. Label the columns as appropriate, such as Date, Time, Caffeine Usage, Amount of Sleep, or Exercise. Pay attention and note behaviors as indicated.

I greeted Sandy in the waiting room on her first visit to see me. She smiled nervously as we walked back to my office. I asked her if she had any trouble finding the building and she said no and that she had been 25 minutes early because she was worried that she would be late. When I asked about how I could help, she told me that she was chronically anxious, but lately it had become worse than usual. When I asked her if she was taking medication she told me she was; her primary care physician prescribed it for her.

Although it doesn't precisely affect therapeutic journaling but is a part of intake, I admit to my bias in favor of psychiatrists over primary care physicians when it comes to prescribing. Almost every psychiatrist I have ever worked with is more knowledgeable about pharmacology and mental health than even the most well-versed primary care physician. It's simply a matter of emphasis in medical training. That said, I strongly urge (but never insist) a client see a psychiatrist for a work-up regarding medication if it is indicated. Sandy did visit with a psychiatrist who felt her current medication and dosage were correct.

Sandy had also had a recent physical exam, so both physical and medication concerns could be ruled out. In the course of reviewing her history and biographical statement, I learned that several other members of her family had issues with anxiety.

The next area I addressed was lifestyle. I asked Sandy about her exercise routine, her diet, use of alcohol and recreational drugs, the amount of caffeine she ingested, and her sleep patterns. She mentioned that generally she had "pretty healthy habits," but lately she had noticed she had increased her usual amount of caffeine, she was sleeping less than usual, and her personal fitness routine had fallen by the wayside.

I suggested that she track the amount of caffeine, her sleep schedule, and her fitness routine for a few weeks so we could evaluate it together. I provided a blank tracking sheet. Since she reported generally being consistent in most of her habits, I asked her what might be causing the current change. After some discussion it became clear to me that the core of her current issue, though originating at work, had now begun to affect her relationships within her family.

Exercises such as the Worry Log and Health Tracking, although quite simple in format, are highly effective tools for keeping track of health and other issues. When Sandy brought her Health Tracking sheets to her next session, she already knew what she needed to do. Even just glancing at the pages, she realized she had been exercising an average of only two days a week instead of her usual five. Most surprising, without realizing it, she had doubled her caffeine usage and was also drinking iced tea and diet sodas later in the day than she had before. Both the lack of exercise and the increase in caffeine had significantly contributed to changes in her sleep pattern.

There had been a number of layoffs at Sandy's company, and she was doing what felt like almost another full-time job, picking up the slack from one of the new vacancies. For the first time since she had started this job four years ago she was bringing work home, cutting into time with her husband and children. Longer days at work prevented Sandy from exercising with more regularity. She had a wonderful summer vacation planned, and now many more vacation hours had been accrued. But in the meantime, Sandy needed to make some changes, soon.

NATURE WALK AND WRITE

If you are feeling anxious or stressed, consider a Nature Walk and Write. Begin by asking yourself a question about something that has been bothering you or has made you feel stuck. Write down the question in your journal or notebook. Next, go outdoors, preferably near water, greenery, or trees. Walk for a few minutes, and then sit quietly. Make notes about thoughts or feelings that come up for you. Continue walking, then sit quietly again and make more notes about your thoughts or feelings.

Because the situation at work was unlikely to change prior to her vacation, Sandy needed to take charge of changing things for herself. Two exercises came to mind to help her. When used regularly, both can reduce stress and anxiety.

The first of these two exercises, Nature Walk and Write, never fails to amaze me. I frequently use it when I teach a full-day workshop and notice energy is waning around mid-afternoon. I sometimes use it when I am working with an individual client who seems to be completely stuck. (I have certainly used it myself many times since beginning this book.) There are four parts to the exercise. Begin by noting what is causing stress, anxiety, or what otherwise may be making you uncomfortable, such as feeling stuck or being unable to answer a question. Next, walk outside. Remaining quiet, walk for several minutes. When you return, make notes in your journal or notebook.

At times I assign Nature Walk and Write as homework, and at other times, I take a few minutes during the session and walk outdoors with a client. To get a feel for a Nature Walk and Write, let's walk along with Sandy. I asked her to write down in her notebook a question about her current stressor. She wrote: "How do I manage my current work stress until I get away on vacation?" Then we took a short walk together around the building. Although there is a large parking lot, there are also flowers, grass, and trees. It was warm outside, and Sandy took off her sandals and walked on the grass. We didn't speak, just walked in companionable silence. I noticed that Sandy's pace had slowed and she began to look more closely at what she saw—an artfully arranged grouping of rocks, a blossom on a cherry tree. I noticed that she had made a small sketch in her notebook. When we returned to my office, she sat for a few minutes and jotted down some notes.

I smiled at her when she looked up. "Well?"

"You know," she said slowly, "I could bring in a few flowers and put them in a small vase on my desk. I also have some beautiful shells I found when I went to the beach a few months ago. I could bring those in, too. Somehow just looking at the flowers and shells will remind me to slow down and breathe. I think I'll be okay."

When anxious or stressed, the last thing we are likely to remember is to stop and take a walk outdoors. That is why, once we are outdoors, it can be a profound physiological shift.

I have yet to see anyone who has not had some kind of perceptual shift, an answer of some sort, or a new idea with this technique.

FANTASY ISLAND

> Become quiet and pay attention to your breathing. Systematically relax your entire body, beginning with the top of your head. When you are fully relaxed, see in your mind's eye an image from your own Fantasy Island. Integrate your senses by seeing, hearing, and feeling what it is like on your Fantasy Island. Leaving your Fantasy Island for just a few minutes, become alert, and write down as much detail as you can about what you have seen, heard, and felt. As an option, you can create a collage; add pictures, or photos to your written notes. Use your notes and pictures as often as needed to help you return to your Fantasy Island.

A television show called *Fantasy Island* ran for seven seasons beginning in 1977. The concept of the series was a romanticized three days on an island wherein the lucky visitor was treated to his or her ultimate fantasy. The Penvisioning exercise I am about to describe combines journaling with a bit of *Fantasy Island*. Similar to Nature Walk and Write, Fantasy Island reduces stress and anxiety through a physiological shift.

To begin, I ask clients if they are willing to close their eyes and participate in a visualization. When I have consent, I ask them to become quiet and pay attention to their breathing. Systematically, I guide them through a full-body progressive relaxation, a standard and established treatment for anxiety. I again make a request for them to pay attention to their breathing.

I ask clients to indicate if they are fully relaxed, usually with a nod to acknowledge the level of relaxation. If clients indicate they are not yet fully relaxed, I might gently move to a hypnotic trance by counting backward or try other interventions of this sort. If you are not trained in hypnotherapy or are not comfortable with this approach, you can continue this part by repeating the progressive relaxation (see Appendix B). When your client is as relaxed as possible, ask them to begin to imagine a scene from their own Fantasy Island. I make a few suggestions such as, "Perhaps you are at a beautiful beach, hiking up a mountain, or napping in a hammock under a shady tree." I ask for a nod of acknowledgment once the location for the visualization has been established. I integrate all the senses by asking clients to notice what they can see, hear, touch, and even smell. When I check in to make sure clients are fully present in their Fantasy Island visualization, I suggest they take several minutes to continue to enjoy the sensations they are experiencing.

After that, I gently guide them to return to the present and alert themselves to the surroundings of my office. I ask them to write rapidly, describing the scenario they have witnessed. I remind them they can drop back into their Fantasy Island any time they want. The more frequently they are able to drop back in, the easier it becomes to return to the present and drop back in again. Each time clients go back into their relaxed state, they are remembering both the physical sensation and the visual image of relaxation. I remind the client to jot down any additional details they have noticed.

For some clients it is sufficient to have learned to do progressive relaxation combined with visualization and then writing down the experience. Writing about the experience and describing their Fantasy Island in detail helps imprint the imagery. The more the exercise is practiced, the better and more easily it becomes available when needed.

For others, I add an additional step. I ask them to continue to practice relaxation and use their notes to guide them, then I add that for their homework, they should find a photo, a picture in a magazine representing their Fantasy Island, or if they have time and energy for it, create a collage.

Whether it presents as generalized anxiety disorder, panic attacks, or social anxiety, we know anxiety can be debilitating. With careful interventions and medication evaluation, it can be well managed.

CHAPTER *8*

Depression and Mood Disorders

*A*t one time or another, we have all experienced the occasional sadness of everyday life, what we might refer to as "feeling a little down" or "feeling a little blue." Consider this scenario if you have never personally experienced clinical depression:

I don't exactly know what's wrong, but I know something is off. Lately, nothing has been any fun. As a matter of fact I can't remember the last time I did have fun. The word <u>fun</u> even sounds foreign, as though I have forgotten what it means. I have very low energy, and admit only to myself that several mornings a week, I can barely get out of bed. I feel exhausted and am not sleeping well at night. I fall asleep but wake up at 1 or 2 in the morning, wide awake and unable to go back to sleep. I am overeating even though I know I am not *hungry. I know I should be more active, but I don't have the energy to exercise. I feel overwhelmed with tasks and things I need to do, but I don't really feel like doing anything. I have a vague sense that nothing will make me happy and there is nothing I am looking forward to.*

The word *depression* is used so frequently in general conversation that sometimes it's hard to distinguish the difference between being a little down and the actual psychological disorder of depression as indicated by the foregoing journal entry. I think perhaps more than any other psychological disorder, depression can be one of the most difficult to understand. There is a tendency (unfortunately even among our colleagues) to imagine depression is something you can just "snap out of."

Something of a paradox exists in terms of the therapeutic value of journaling for healing depression. Severe depression, such as an episode of major depressive disorder, can make journaling extremely challenging, although not impossible. On the other hand, many people with mild depression are drawn to journaling. Anecdotally, many clients and students I have worked with over the years report they journal only when they are depressed.

In this chapter I focus on depression ranging from mild depression to major depressive disorder. The exercises will represent a wide range of treatment focus, such as support, cathartic, cognitive, and insight-providing methods (Badal, 2006).

THREE GOOD THINGS

Each night before bed, sit quietly and think about the good things that happened during the day. Write down three good things in a journal or notebook. Do this every day for at least a month. Notice how this exercise makes you feel, and at the end of a month, write about that.

It is difficult to say where gratitude lists originated. They have become inordinately popular over the last decade due in part to Oprah Winfrey and authors such as Sarah Ban Breathnach, who wrote *Simple Abundance* (1995). But gratitude is not just a pop psychology notion. The emerging field of evidence-based positive psychology suggests that depression is one of several clinical diagnoses that respond well to specific positive psychology interventions (Sin and Lyubomirsky, 2009). One such intervention cited by leading researcher Martin Seligman and his colleagues is Three Good Things (Seligman, Steen, Park, and Peterson, 2005).

In this exercise, three things for which one is grateful are listed in a journal or notebook each evening. I have used this exercise with many clients, but one that stands out is the case of Janice. Janice was a librarian, very close to retirement. I had worked with her intermittently over the years, but her current bout of depression was of particular concern. She had been diagnosed with cyclothymic disorder many years ago. She generally kept her depression stabilized with the careful use of well-managed antidepressant medication. But with retirement just a few months away, Janice had reached an especially low point. Fortunately, she was generally compliant and had worked with me long enough to trust my suggested interventions, although she remained skeptical. I explained Three Good Things to her.

"Each evening I would like you to sit down for a few minutes and think about three good things that happened during the day," I began. "Then, in your journal or in a notebook, write down those three things."

"What if I can't think of three things?" asked Janice. "What if I can only think of two, or even just one?" I said that I understood this could be challenging, but it was important to come up with three things even though it might require a bit of effort. It didn't matter what the three things were or how minor they might seem, because this was more about learning to focus on things that had gone well. Janice looked at me skeptically, but said she would try.

When she returned two weeks later, Janice had followed up with her list 10 out of 14 days. Here is a sampling of what she showed me:

- I got my taxes done.
- My neighbor invited me over for dinner.
- My daughter called and we had a nice phone conversation.
- I cleaned out my front hall closet.
- I found a book I thought I had lost.
- Two flowers bloomed in my back yard.

I asked what the experience had been like for her, and Janice said that in some ways it was more difficult than she had anticipated, but in other ways, it was easier. "How so?" I asked.

She explained that it had been challenging to come up with good things on some days. But she also said that once she started looking for good things that had happened, it became easier to notice them. In a nutshell, that is the purpose of this exercise: to retrain the perspective and look for positive things to happen.

VOICING YOUR DEPRESSION

Sit quietly for at least five minutes. Become aware of your breathing. Become aware of your body. Allow any sensations or feelings to surface. When you are ready, write about what feelings have come up.

Nancy, a 57-year-old high school principal, came to see me shortly after she had separated from her husband, Jake. They had been married 35 years, raised children together, and had full and active lives. Once the children were out of the house and out on their own, she and Jake acknowledged what they had not wanted to admit—their marriage had been over for some time. Although many couples find a renewed connection once the last child has left the nest, others experience just the opposite.

On the job, Nancy was highly competent. She handled challenges with everything from difficult students and faculty members to department budgets with proficiency and skill. But although she was used to a high level of professional stress, the separation was providing stress of a different kind. When Nancy came home at the end of her workday she suddenly found herself feeling exhausted and drained. Normally she would have prepared dinner for her husband, gone back to school for an evening meeting, gone to her book club meeting, or done paperwork at the dining room table for a few hours after dinner.

I discussed with Nancy that what she was likely experiencing was depression, which was a part of her grief process. No one had died, but she was nonetheless experiencing the death of the marriage. I asked if she was willing to do some writing about her feelings. I was well aware that Nancy didn't have a lot of extra energy and was just trying to get through the day. She agreed, however, that she could probably write for a few minutes a day. I recommended she set a timer for 10 minutes and if possible write in the morning. I suggested she sit for a moment and as much as she could just allow her feelings to surface.

When I saw Nancy next, she shared with me part of what she had written over the course of several days:

I remember a book from a long time ago. I always thought it was a funny title: Been Down So Long it Looks Like Up to Me. I was never really sure exactly what it meant, but somehow that's how I feel—like somehow I've fallen into some deep dark hole and I will never be able to crawl my way out. It's like the sun is blocked and all I see is the cover of dark clouds, threatening, like before a rainstorm.

The grayness lingers. I feel as if I am walking through molasses, every step is exhausting. A part of me just wants to curl up in a little ball and cry. I'm just afraid if I start crying, I'll never stop.

How could this have happened to us? When did it happen? Was there some moment in time when every- thing changed? If so, I don't recall—we were too busy with the kids, with our lives. Maybe it's like a tire with a tiny puncture. You're rolling along fine, then one day you go out and start the car and the tire is flat—like our marriage. We ignored the maintenance on the car, and slowly all the air leaked out.

In my experience, most of us will do just about anything to avoid the actual feeling of being depressed. The reason an exercise such as Voicing Your Depression works is that it does just the opposite— it confronts the depression head on. The fear of experiencing depression can be worse than actually feeling it.

GIVING DEPRESSION A VOICE

Sit quietly for a few moments. Become aware of your breathing. Become aware of your body. Begin to imagine your depression has a voice. Listen, and write down what you hear.

Nancy was an intelligent and logical woman. She was excellent at problem solving for others, but when it came to being aware of her own feelings, she was at a bit of a loss. I was impressed by what she shared with me in the passages just quoted. It occurred to me that there might be a slight variation on Voicing Your Depression that she might try. I explained to her what projection meant, encouraging her to write from the perspective of the depression.

Here is part of what Nancy wrote:

*I am Nancy's depression and I'll tell you what—I'm
getting damn sick of these dark clouds and all this
stuck-in-molasses stuff. You want to know what I'm
feeling? I'm feeling mad, I mean really pissed off and
angry. I'm tired of moping around and feeling sorry for
myself. I want to talk about that husband of yours. This
isn't exactly what I had in mind for you at this point
in your life. You kept growing, going to school, taking
classes, moving ahead and he just kind of stayed where
he was. This should be the time of life when you are free
to do what you want; you've gotten through the hard
stuff and this should be the fun time—but it's not and it
sucks.*

Although it's always hard to anticipate how a client will respond to any given journaling exercise, Nancy surprised both of us. Since it had been years since she had done any personal journaling, she hadn't expected very much would happen. But I think a great deal happened.

In the first exercise, Voicing Your Depression, Nancy was able to allow feelings to surface she didn't even know were there. Acknowledging feelings is the beginning of healing. At first glance, Giving Depression a Voice sounds as though it's the same thing as Voicing Your Depression, but it is different in a subtle way. With the first exercise, Nancy was able to get in touch with her feelings. With the second exercise, using projection as a vehicle, she was able to go more deeply into the feeling, allowing the underlying anger to surface.

Most important about the use of these two exercises is that one may work for a client and another one may work decidedly better. Or one may not work at all and simply fall flat. Move on and try something else. Or start with any of the exercises you find throughout this book and change or tweak the suggestions to work for your client.

There is a certain amount of trial and error when trying various approaches. Don't be discouraged. Keep at it.

I DON'T WANT LIST

At a time when you are feeling down or out of sorts, sit down and think about all the things you don't want to do. Begin making a list. Add all the things you can think of: things you know you don't want to do, things you feel you should do but still don't want to do, and things someone else feels you should do. When the list feels complete for the moment, notice how you feel. Spend some time writing about that.

A different approach to helping your client get in touch with anger that may be buried under the surface of depression is a type of Quick List I call the I Don't Want List. (This is one of my favorite journaling exercises.) Though it works well with a client who is depressed, it also works well for just being in a grouchy or foul mood. In fact, that's how I discovered how it worked.

One particular day, many years ago, I didn't feel like going to the office. I didn't feel like emptying the dishwasher. I didn't feel like doing much of anything I was supposed to be doing. I thought I would write in my journal, and even that made me grouchy. So I started to make a list of all the things I didn't want to do. The list kept getting longer. After a few minutes I realized I was having a good time. Not only that, I was actually feeling energized.

Here's how I used the I Don't Want List with Brody. He was 17 years old. Even though I don't usually see children or teens in my practice, I do occasionally see the child of an ongoing client. Brody's mother brought him in, explaining that his grades had dropped considerably in the last semester and she was concerned something was wrong. After seeing the expression on Brody's face in the waiting room, I wasn't looking forward to the session. After a few minutes of monosyllabic responses to my questions, I asked if he would be willing to create a list of all the things he didn't want to do. He shrugged. "Do you want to write, or should I write down what you want on the list?"

Brody responded that he would do the writing himself. I handed him a tablet of paper and a pen. He closed his eyes, and I thought he had fallen asleep, but then he started writing. Slowly at first, then picking up speed as he went, Brody started his list. When he was done he handed me the clipboard. On his list he had included:

- I don't want to go to German class. I hate it and I don't see the point.
- I don't want to work in my dad's shop.
- I don't want to go back east and visit my grandmother.
- I don't want to do any family trips. I'm way too old for that.
- I don't want to clean my room. It's my room, why can't I leave it the way I want it?
- I don't want any more "life lessons" from Dad.

After writing, Brody opened up and told me more about the things he didn't want, as well as some of the things he wanted. He did have some understandable family pressure to keep up his grades, do his college applications for early decision, and work part-time. He had some mild depression but he was also suffering from "senioritis," a disorder whose known course was resolved by graduation.

INTENTIONAL ACTIVITIES LOG

> To keep track of intentional activities to lessen depression, begin a written log. Entries don't need to be long, just write down the essential points, summarizing the results of your intentional activities and your feelings. Use this log as a reference point to look back and see the power of your intentions.

Rebecca was a new client of mine, recently diagnosed with dysthymia. During intake I learned that she was not the only one in her family diagnosed with depression. Her mother, grandmother, and one of her sisters all experienced some form of depression. Although Rebecca was certainly not happy with her diagnosis, she was willing to do what she could to minimize the effect depression had on her life.

As I frequently do when working with a client with depression, I drew a circle in the center of a page of a large sketch tablet and divided it into eight sections. I suggested to Rebecca that there were many components, or pieces of the pie, as it were, that contributed to depression. Although depression itself was beyond our control, many healing aspects of depression were well within our control.

First, states neuroscientist Leonie Welberg, "Many depression and anxiety disorders are better treated with a combination of psychotherapy and antidepressant drugs" (Welberg, 2012). Second, Sonia Lyubomirsky, a leading researcher in positive psychology, reports that there are several evidence-based activities that she calls intentional activities—behaviors that can be done to help people feel better, which includes such things as appreciation, avoidance of negative thinking, diet, exercise, kindness to others, meditation, and personal goal setting (Lyubomirsky, 2008). These activities can be easily supported with journaling.

Figure 8.1 indicates a number of intentional activities. Remember, intentional activities are those activities we choose to do purposely in an effort to feel better.

INTENTIONAL ACTIVITIES LOG

In Chapter 7 I discussed keeping a Health Log. This type of log is formatted as a chart, like a spreadsheet. But another type of log is narrative in format. For example, I asked Rebecca to track several of

FIGURE 8.1

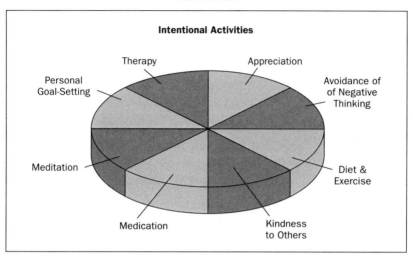

her intentional behaviors by simply making brief notes of what she noticed. Not all intentional behaviors work for everyone. Help your client select those activities of interest to him or her, explaining that deliberately doing these activities will help in mollifying depression. Rebecca chose to work specifically with kindness to others and avoiding negative thinking. Here is what she wrote in her log:

Avoidance of Negative Thinking: I wasn't quite sure about this; I mean if I could avoid negative thinking, I wouldn't be depressed, right? But then I realized what that really meant for me is that I don't have to watch the endless news loops on CNN so I kept hearing negative newscasts over and over. Now I watch the news for 10 minutes once a day—it's really all I need to know.

Kindness to Others: Honestly, I didn't have any idea about this activity either. I don't mean to be selfish, but how does kindness to others benefit me? So as an experiment, I joined a volunteer program in my church that takes meals to shut-ins. It's only a few hours a week, but I always feel better after I do it. I stop whining and feeling sorry for myself and put my attention on someone else.

At one point, Rebecca needed to leave town for several days for a business trip. I asked her if she had some specific goals for the trip that she might want to focus on. Of course she had her business agenda, and I asked her if she had any personal goals for herself, something that was challenging for her but not overly difficult. She told me she would think about it, although she had nothing specific in mind.

The next week we talked again about the trip. Rebecca had made some notes in her Intentional Activities Log. This is what she wrote:

These don't seem like big things, but they are important to me. I wanted to challenge myself because when I travel it's especially easy to let things go. The first thing I did was that I actually used the gym in the hotel. I always pack gym clothes and tell myself I'll use them, but this time I really did. Twice! The other personal goal I set for myself was to deal with the rental car. I usually try to get someone else to do it, but this time I volunteered. I was really proud of myself because using my phone app I managed to get myself around.

I agree with Rebecca that although these may not seem like big things, the issue here is the sense of accomplishment. The successful completion of selected activities can significantly shift mood and enhance positive sense of self.

SMALL STEPS

On a new page in your journal or a notebook, create two columns, or simply draw a line down the middle of a page. Each time you accomplish even a small thing, write down the date on the left hand side of the page. Opposite the date on the right side, describe what you accomplished, using just a few words. Use this log as a reference point, as needed.

In 1991, Richard Dreyfus and Bill Murray starred in a film called *What About Bob?* Although the movie was popular, it was the kind of film that makes therapists cringe at the portrayal of the egotistical and boundary-challenged psychiatrist. One of the plot points was about a book the therapist had written called *Baby Steps*; the concept was that changes happen in very small increments. The concept of baby or small steps works very well for depression, especially a major depressive episode.

If you are working with a client suffering from a major depressive episode, about the only thing you can do is take small steps. Anything more can be overwhelming. By creating a very simple method of recording, clients can track small, incremental steps. Suggest to your client that he or she set up two columns, one listing the date and the other listing the small step taken. You might suggest they need to use only a few words.

Deb, a client who had recurring depressive episodes, had done this exercise before and knew how to keep track using only a few words. Here is a sample of what she wrote:

- 3/2 Called psychiatrist to schedule medication evaluation
- 3/3 Made grocery list and purchased five items
- 3/5 Washed one load of clothes

Symptoms of depression can range from mildly bothersome to intensely incapacitating, from acute to chronic. Journalist and news commentator Jane Pauley revealed, "I didn't suffer the misconception that depression was all in my head or a mark of poor character. I knew it was a disease, and, like all diseases, was treatable" (McPhee, 2008). Useful treatments we have looked at in this chapter are positive psychology interventions (Three Good Things and Intentional Activities Log), anger awareness and release (Voicing Your Depression, Giving Depression a Voice, and the I Don't Want List), and raising mood by acknowledging progress, no matter how incremental (Small Steps).

CHAPTER 9

Grief and Mourning

*S*everal years ago on a summer afternoon, I met Marla for the first time. We walked up the hallway from the lobby into my office, chatting about the weather. She had an impish grin and a mass of unruly dark curls, beginning to gray at the temples.

The moment I closed the door and Marla sat down, she burst into tears. "I told myself I wouldn't cry," she said as a fresh wave of sobbing began. I waited a few moments and then gently urged her to continue with what she had told me two days ago on the phone.

"My aunt," she began, "just found out she has pancreatic cancer. It's too advanced for surgery and she doesn't have much time. I can't believe it! How could this happen?" The words poured out in a rush. "It's just that she has always been more of a mother to me than an aunt." I nodded and Marla continued. "She's the only family I have left."

Marla's maternal grandparents had raised her after the death of her parents when she was nine. Over the years her grandparents and her aunt formed a close-knit family for her. Marla had grown exceptionally close to her aunt. Because she wanted to attend to her aunt's needs in the coming weeks, I scheduled her return for the following month.

Her beloved aunt died soon after her diagnosis. Marla was distraught over this loss. She reported bouts of crying throughout the day, feeling "blue" and "down in the dumps," trouble sleeping, and sometimes oversleeping. As I considered the treatment plan for her, I knew that I would need to bear in mind both Marla's adjustment to her loss and an important underlying component of grief work—fear of forgetting the deceased. I knew how draining the grief process could be, so whatever direction I chose, it would be necessary to proceed gently and with care. Therapeutic journaling would be a good treatment. Writing supports adjustment to loss by unfolding at its own pace as well as offering a way to record and process memories.

UNCOMPLICATED GRIEF

In this section on uncomplicated grief, I divide the grief process into three phases—facing the truth, anger and depression, and becoming whole again. As Marla began to face the reality of her aunt's death, I introduced four therapeutic journaling exercises over a period of several weeks. These exercises use a list format, which requires less focus than writing complete sentences. Even in uncomplicated grief, the client simply does not possess the energy, focus, or stamina to do big chunks of writing. When a client is grief-stricken, severely depressed, ill, or otherwise incapacitated, therapeutic journaling can still be indicated, but it's best to keep assignments short and simple.

Keep in mind that the purpose of any therapeutic journaling for the client should be designed to continue, deepen, and enhance the work from the session.

Structuring the Session

Although a session doesn't follow a script, most follow somewhat of a pattern. The first part is connecting, which may include rapport building if this is a client I don't yet know or a check-in if it is an ongoing client. The opening connection is like an introduction, building a bridge between the prior visit and the current one. During that time, I may check with the client to see whether any significant events have occurred, how well the client has been functioning, or if the client has a high-priority issue they want to address during the session. I have found that these few minutes at the beginning of the session helps focus the client and set the agenda. If a client is particularly unfocused or agitated, adding a brief meditation or sitting quietly with eyes closed can also be calming.

The second or middle part of the session is when the primary work of therapy takes place. This may include open-ended questions, careful reflective listening, a supportive conversation, or any other means to deepen the issue that the client is working on. In Marla's case, because she had such a close relationship with her aunt and the death was so recent, she was able to access her feelings easily. For her, this segment of the sessions included my providing information about the grieving process in an effort to normalize her feelings.

The third or concluding part of the session is when the salient points of the session are summarized. At this point the transition from the work of the session segues to recommended journaling exercises. Remember, that the purpose of assigned therapeutic journaling is to enhance the value of the session by continuing and deepening the client's process following the session.

LOVING MEMORY LIST

> Begin your Loving Memory List by sitting alone, quietly, in a place where you will not be disturbed. Think of the person you have lost and pay attention to your feelings. When you are ready, begin writing a list of loving memories of the person you have lost. Write quickly; don't stop to edit or rewrite anything. When you have written several memories, go back and add as much detail as you can to them.

As the work with Marla proceeded, she frequently shared memories about her aunt, leading quite naturally to the first exercise, Loving Memory List. During the first two months after her aunt's death, Marla's emotions were too raw to attempt any homework other than experiencing her grief. After that time, I asked if she would be willing to try a very brief journaling exercise. She agreed to do so.

For the Loving Memory List, I asked Marla to take some time during the week to sit quietly and begin a list of memories about her aunt. She was to add to the list as a new memory came to her. At this point, the focus was on simply gathering memories. Marla's Loving Memory List began like this:

- My aunt's worn black scarf
- The scent of her Chanel perfume
- How she would look at me intently, listening to every word I said
- How loving and welcoming she always was to my friends

As she became more comfortable with this exercise over a few weeks, I asked her to add detail to each of the memories. For example, in describing her aunt's scarf, she wrote, "I loved her soft, fuzzy black scarf with the worn patches. When I was young, I would sneak it out of the hallway closet when she visited. I felt so grown up when I wrapped it around my neck, with its lingering scent of my aunt's favorite Chanel perfume."

My purpose in directing Marla to add details to the memories was not for literary reasons, but for psychological healing. Written details, such as the memory and description of the scarf and her memory of wearing it, provide concrete details and complete a partial memory. Paradoxically, by making the memory whole and therefore being able to momentarily relive it, Marla could begin to lovingly release her pain and begin to heal. Also, by writing down her memories, she began to get a glimpse that although her aunt was no longer in her life physically, she was still an important presence.

During the first three months of Marla's work with me, I intro- duced her to two more exercises called Photographic Memories and Memories from Objects. Both of these exercises incorporate the use of props and can be integrated into the Loving Memory List. Photos are particularly poignant during grief work, as are objects. The objects may be small, such as a button, a pen, or a small toy, or larger, such as a book or an article of clothing. The purpose of gathering photos and objects is to help memories surface. There should be no limits placed on the client as to what is selected as meaningful. Memories are highly personal.

Marla brought photos and objects with her in a small bag. She talked about each item during the session, sometimes with a slight smile and sometimes quietly and tearfully. For example, she brought in a tiny plastic duck she kept on her desk. It represented a sweet moment from years ago when she and her aunt had talked about getting their ducks in a row. A simple photograph could bring up several different memories, such as a birthday or holiday. At the close of each session, I suggested that Marla continue these exercises on her own, adding to her Loving Memory List.

PHOTOGRAPHIC MEMORIES

When you have some quiet, uninterrupted time alone, select several photographs of the person you have lost. Use the photos to help jar your memory, but go beyond just the visual images in the photos. Remember scents, tastes, sounds, and feelings. Close your eyes. Let yourself drift back in time, remembering. You may want to add some notes to your Loving Memory List.

MEMORIES FROM OBJECTS

In the same way that you have used photographs to create memories, you can also use objects—a souvenir, a trinket, or other small object. Allow the objects to help you go back in time and remember what you can about the person you have lost. Add your notes to your Loving Memory List.

I WISH I COULD TELL YOU LIST

Begin by sitting quietly for a few minutes. When you are ready, take a moment to recall the loved one you are thinking about. Consider what you would like to tell him or her if it was possible to do so. As you become aware of things you would have liked to say, jot them down. Remember, no subject is too big and no detail too small to share with someone who would have cared.

As Marla continued to process her memories, she began to express a deep longing to talk to her aunt. She had reached a point common in the early stage of grief—an overwhelming desire to talk to or share information about your current life with the deceased. It can be a devastating feeling, and the void can be very painful. I devised a second exercise for her, which I called the I Wish I Could Tell You List.

Marla frequently described current situations expressing the sentiment, "If only I could just call her up and tell her this," or "She would have loved this so much." I began by asking her to describe specifically what she wanted to tell her aunt. She flushed slightly and said she wanted to tell her aunt about the relationship with a man in her office that had begun six months earlier. She also wanted her aunt to know how much she missed their weekly "girlfriend" lunch dates. Because fear of forgetting can block the processing of grief, both a Loving Memory List and an I Wish I Could Tell You List help by preserving such memories. This allows the client to let go without forgetting.

A variation on the I Wish I Could Tell You List is to have the client imagine she is writing a letter to her loved one. For example, a woman who lost her husband might write a series of letters in her journal, describing ordinary, everyday events—shopping, a movie she had seen, or a book she had read. The need to write an I Wish I Could Tell You Letter diminishes after time; but I have seen many clients comforted by this type of writing.

I WISH I COULD TELL YOU LETTER

Begin by sitting quietly for a few minutes. When you are ready, take a moment to recall the loved one you are thinking about and consider what you would like to tell him or her in a letter if it was possible to do so.

As Marla began to experience feelings of anger, a normal and pre-dictable part of the grief process, I introduced an additional exercise, an Angry List. One of the most difficult parts of grief work is ownership of anger. It is a confusing sentiment to have toward someone you love. The client may feel hurt, lonely, abandoned, depressed, or afraid, and these emotions frequently exhibit as anger. On the other hand, it can also be difficult to express anger. Becoming angry at someone you loved can bring up feelings of guilt—How can I be angry at someone who died? I suggested to Marla that even if anger didn't make "sense," to write down what she felt on her Angry List. Even though this was difficult for her, she wrote such things, as "I'm angry because you abandoned me," and "I'm angry because my family is gone," and finally, "I feel guilty for saying this, but you have left me alone."

ANGRY LIST

Imagine having a conversation with the loved one you have lost. Allow yourself to write down everything that makes you angry with him or her. Even if doing this is difficult and brings up feelings of guilt, stay with it. These feelings are temporary and an important part of healing.

FORGIVENESS LETTER

Find a time when you will not be interrupted. Become quiet and let your breathing slow. Close your eyes and visualize the person you are now ready to forgive. Begin writing your letter, saying everything you need to say to forgive.

An exercise I didn't use with Marla but have used with other clients who are struggling to process grief is the Forgiveness Letter. It didn't apply to Marla because of the emotional closeness and physical proximity she had enjoyed with her aunt. They had lunch together on a weekly basis, so most things in the relationship were fairly current; there was little left unfinished.

In cases where there has been unfinished business, the Forgiveness Letter can provide significant healing. For example, Elizabeth, a client who had experienced a difficult relationship with her estranged husband, James, would never have imagined forgiving him while he was alive. They had separated shortly after James began a series of brief affairs while traveling abroad for five months. After returning home from his travels, he had been killed in a car accident.

It was a difficult path for Elizabeth. She still loved James, in spite
of their marital difficulties. At times she wondered if her feelings of
sadness and anger would ever end.

At my suggestion, Elizabeth began a series of letters to James. She
wrote the letters as though she was speaking to him directly, pouring
her feelings out on paper. She wrote: "How could you have done this
to me? Don't you think I was lonely, too? Don't you think I missed
our time together, holding each other and talking about every little
detail of our day until we fell asleep? I was lonely too, but I never
cheated on you! How could you do this to me?"

Eventually, she worked through her anger, coming to understand painfully how she and James had both caused the emotional
distance between them. Through the course of the letters, she learned
that forgiveness is not the same as forgetting. Over a year after his
death, she remained sad about the loss of her husband, with holidays,
their birthdays, and their anniversary being especially difficult. But
Elizabeth was able to forgive James eventually. Her Forgiveness Letter
listed all of the ways she had been hurt in the marriage, but she was
also now able to write about what had been good. She was eventually
able to work through the phases of grief and come to a place of peace.

Elizabeth was eventually able to write the following Forgiveness
Letter:

James,
I have certainly spent a lot of time expressing my anger
toward you. But there were also good times and many
sweet moments with you over the years. I remember
your gentleness and kindness, not just with me, but with
practically everyone you knew. I was so angry when I
found out about the affairs. But as time has gone by, I
see how we both had begun to drift apart. Marriage takes
so much more effort than either of us ever imagined. I
miss you and wish we had found a way to reconcile.

There is no easy way through the process of recovering after a loss. Each client must take his or her own time and path. Although therapeutic journaling is not intended to replace psychotherapy, it can be a powerful adjunct to good clinical work. Writing is a way of continuing the session and keeping continuity between sessions, as well as keeping the progress of the work moving forward.

COMPLICATED GRIEF

What happens when a client is unable to move from acute grief to integrated grief? At what point does the process of bereavement shift from uncomplicated grief to complicated grief (Zisook and Shear, 2009)? The two terms themselves need some explanation. *Uncomplicated grief* refers to the process of anticipated mourning we are most familiar with—the Kübler-Ross model (Kübler-Ross, 1973)—in which denial, anger, bartering, and depression eventually lead to acceptance. In complicated grief, on the other hand, the grief process becomes blocked or stuck. It fails to make the expected transition from acute grief to integrated grief. That is not to say that any grief is easy. Grief is complex in any form. However, what makes complicated grief so difficult is that it is often hard to distinguish from major depression. Because grieving and depression may look alike in terms of symptoms, major depression may be overlooked. Such was the case in my work with Alan.

Alan, age 42, came to see me six months after his father died. He presented with sleep difficulties, vivid nightmares, weight loss, low energy, and mental confusion while in his workplace, doing tasks he had done repeatedly for years. As we spoke further, he revealed more of his family history and background, and it became clearer as to why he continued to suffer so intensely in his grieving. His father's death had precipitated an episode of major depression. Alan had struggled with depression his whole adult life, and the trauma of his father's death brought up memories he had worked hard to suppress.

Alan had grown up in a small Midwestern town where his father served as a deacon of the church, coached soccer, and had served his community as a volunteer firefighter. His father appeared to friends and neighbors as the perfect dad, and he was well liked and highly regarded by friends and neighbors. But his behavior was quite different in the privacy of his own home. With his own family, Alan's father would often turn moody and taciturn. He spoke little and most nights drank heavily, lashing out physically at Alan's mother and younger brother for anything he considered to be a slight, even though the insults were largely imagined. In an effort to protect them, Alan had often received the brunt of his father's anger and on several occasions had gone to sleep both physically and emotionally beaten. Eventually his mother left her husband, but not before Alan was profoundly affected by the abuse.

In the ensuing years, he had little contact with his father. Hearing from his brother that their father had died suddenly, Alan was confronted with myriad emotions. He felt sad—less so about his father's death than about the childhood he had never had. He felt guilty because even though he understood why, he responded reluctantly or sometimes not at all when his father reached out to him in his recent sobriety.

Whereas Marla had a relatively uncomplicated path on her journey of healing from the loss of her aunt, Alan's situation was complex. Before he could even begin to resolve his ambivalence at the death of his father, he needed to confront the trauma of his abusive childhood. Although reluctant at first, believing "it wouldn't do any good," he began journaling in between sessions. I specifically asked him to describe as much as he could remember about the incidents with his father. Alan was to write continuously for at least 20 minutes four times a week without regard to spelling, syntax, or punctuation using a free-form approach.

The use of free-form writing had several purposes here. First, although the process was rigorous and at times stressful, Alan was able to make use of an important principle found by researchers. By writing authentically about previously undisclosed trauma, he was able to integrate (rather than continue to inhibit) the negative emotions he had long suppressed about his father. He was also able to construct a more meaningful, organized narrative about the events of his childhood. The creation of such a narrative from fragments of memory is important in that translating traumatic experiences into language brings understanding and eventually allows the trauma to dissipate (Pennebaker, 1997). A part of one such writing session follows:

> *Write about my dad—oh crap, I don't even like to call him "Dad," because he wasn't. How could he have been a dad? He was a monster! More like Jekyll and Hyde. That's the part that really hurt the most. How could this monster be a perfectly nice guy to everyone but the people he was supposed to have loved the most? I wanted so much for him to be the person he was when he wasn't drinking, that was the dad I loved, not that monster.*

Once Alan began writing, specific details occurred to him. He wrote of the physical pain and rage:

> *It was like he was no longer human. He lost all sense of what he was doing. He just kept hitting me like I was a punching bag. It seemed like hours had passed, even though I knew it was only seconds. And then I felt something I had never felt before. I couldn't even have described it at the time. Now I know it was rage. My own anger at how this man, this usually kind, loving man, fueled by alcohol could become someone else entirely. It was this man I wanted to kill, this man who gave me the strength to fight back.*

There is an important word of caution in using this writing paradigm. Unfortunately, an immediate side effect of expressive writing that is negative in tone is that the client will feel worse for a short time after. It is not dissimilar to clients who try to avoid crying during a session. Crying, expressive writing, or any other highly emotive experience can leave the client feeling drained, exhausted, and moderately depressed. However, this side effect is temporary, and after a brief recovery period, the client will feel considerably better. Let the client know about the potential to feel poorly for a short while, but don't give it undue emphasis. Emphasize instead how expressing emotion in fact leads to healing of trauma.

Despite the momentary discomfort this emotional expression creates, there is another benefit. We found that through Alan's writing, specific target memories could be recovered and through EMDR in particular and other, more traditional forms of therapy, these target memories provided important details. For example, when Alan was able to target the memory of his father beating him, he was able to process his own awakened strength and how he had used it to survive.

Alan continued his work with me for several months. Did he ever recover from the double challenge of healing his traumatic childhood as well as the eventual grief at his father's death? In his own words, "What I have learned is that forgiving is not the same as forgetting."

I strongly recommend that the use of journaling as an adjunct to psychotherapy be used carefully. It is essential to integrate journaling into an overall well-designed treatment plan, including a medication evaluation if indicated or the use of outside resources such as twelve-step programs and other such support groups.

CHAPTER *10*

Low Self-Esteem

*I*n the last three chapters I discussed anxiety, depression, and grief—
all diagnoses that have symptoms that are reasonably clear-cut and relatively easy to identify. Low self-esteem is not necessarily as obvious.
Clients are less likely to enter your office commenting that there is
a problem with low self-esteem or stating something like "I'm not
feeling good about myself." Nonetheless, we know the powerful effect
low self-esteem has on personal feelings and subsequent behavior. I
am struck by what Nathaniel Branden says about self-esteem:

> *I cannot think of a single psychological difficulty—from anxiety*
> *and depression, to fear of intimacy or of success, to alcohol or*
> *drug abuse, to underachievement at school or at work, to spouse*
> *battering or child molestation, to sexual dysfunctions or emotional*
> *immaturity, to suicide or crimes of violence—that is not traceable*
> *to poor self-esteem (Branden, 1995, p. xv)*

Therapists know how profoundly influenced our clients are
by early childhood experiences. When discussing the impact of
childhood with a client, I frequently stand up on one side of my
office and using the width of the room as a metaphor for a lifetime,
take a giant step across the room. I explain that if you are lucky and
have had particularly good parenting, you are a giant step ahead
on your life journey. The rest of us, I explain as I step back to the
wall, just need to work a little harder. In this chapter I make several
suggestions for integrating the use of therapeutic journaling for
improving self-esteem, especially for clients who have not had the
benefit of good parenting.

THREE GOOD THINGS PLUS

> Each night before bed, sit quietly and think about the good things
> that happened during the day. Write down three good things in a
> journal or notebook. For each event listed, write down your part
> in making this good thing happen. Do this every evening for at
> least two weeks. At the end of two weeks' time, notice how this
> exercise has made you feel and write about that.

In Chapter 8, when I discussed journaling interventions for
depression, I mentioned the use of Three Good Things. If you recall,
Three Good Things asks your client to identify three positive events
that occurred on any particular day. The purpose of the exercise is to
shift perspective from focus on negative to focus on positive outcome
of events. By adding a causative piece to this exercise, Three Good
Things can become additionally useful as Three Good Things Plus. In
other words, when I ask a client to identify three positive things that
happened on any given day, I also ask the client to state their personal
involvement in creating the event (Seligman et al., 2005).

Renee was a 43-year-old woman who had been struggling intermittently with low self-esteem after an on-the-job injury had put
her on disability. I asked her to write down three good things that
happened each day. In addition I asked her to write down how she
contributed to each event or what she did to make the event possible. I suggested that it didn't matter how small or uneventful the
occurrence, but that she focus on her contribution. Renee wrote the
following:

Monday

- Good Thing: Made myself get up and eat breakfast
- My Part: Cooked scrambled eggs
- Good Thing: Talked to my brother for the first time in months
- My Part: I initiated the call
- Good Thing: Got through clearing out half of first drawer of file
  cabinet
- My Part: Finally followed through with file clearing project

Tuesday

- Good Thing: Paid all my bills to date
- My Part: Sat down and did it rather than procrastinating
- Good Thing: Took myself out to a movie
- My Part: Made plans and didn't cancel like I usually do
- Good Thing: Made dental appointment
- My Part: Picked up the phone and made the call

Taking these actions out of context, they seem like are minor
shifts in behavior—cooking eggs, making a phone call, clearing out
a file drawer, paying bills, and going to a movie—everyday tasks or
events most of us do without thinking. But if one chronically lives
with the dark cloud of low self-esteem, each action is significant. In
addition, observing and noting such actions on a daily basis has a
cumulative effect.

There are times when this exercise does not go smoothly, and a client responds with something like, "I can barely think of one thing, much less three," or "That just happened, I had nothing to do with it." In that case, break down the task and ask your client to just come up with one thing, not three. Meet your clients where they are. As self-esteem increases, ask the client to do more. It's also fine to let your client know what you observe in their behavior. Gently confront "I had nothing to do with it," with "That's interesting. Here's how I see it . . ."

IDENTIFYING YOUR STRENGTHS

Ask yourself a question you want answered regarding your strengths. You don't need to know the answer beforehand. For example: What do I love to do? What do I do best? I am happiest when I am doing _____? Set a timer and write continuously for 10 minutes. Don't worry about sentence structure, grammar, syntax, or punctuation. Just write. Allow your question to prompt an answer.

Perhaps not even being conscious of it, you may have noticed in yourself or in the actions of your clients that when you are actively using your natural talents or strengths, you feel better about yourself. You are likely to feel more at ease, competent, and confident when you are engaged in something you do well. There are a number of resources you can guide your clients to in this regard. For example, Richard Bolles's Quick Job Hunting Map, the Strong Interest Inventory, the Myers-Briggs Type Indicator, and the Values in Action Survey (see Appendix D for more information).

However, another approach to identifying strengths is through focused free-form writing. Focused free-form writing incorporates the nonrule style of free-form writing, which is freedom from structure, correct syntax, spelling, and punctuation, but is used with a prompt. For example, I might ask a client to write for 10 minutes without stopping in response to any of the following prompts:

- If you had all the money you needed and had no financial concerns, what would you spend your time doing?
- What actions or activities make you feel most excited, vital, and alive?
- Describe your perfect day in detail.
- What feedback do you consistently get from others about your skills and talents?

Carla had been referred by a friend and came to see me because she was feeling unhappy, out of focus, and had very low energy. As we talked, I learned that she felt she was in a dead-end job with no prospects for promotion. She knew she wasn't doing work she loved, but she didn't really know what else she wanted. She believed she needed to stay at her current job to support herself.

Carla worked in an administrative position. Although she was quite competent on the job, the work was not stimulating or challenging to her. She was torn because although she didn't want to be at the job, the salary was quite generous and the benefits were excellent. She wondered: Was that enough? For homework, I suggested Carla spend about 10 minutes a day over the next week journaling about times in her life when she felt she had been doing work she loved, what activities made her really happy, and what she fantasized about spending her time doing.

The following week Carla returned. Here is part of what she had written:

It's hard to imagine what I would do if I didn't have to worry about making a living. My whole life I've only wanted to do three things—I love to read, write, and work with little children. Since I was in middle school, people told me I was gifted with kids. I've been baby-sitting forever; I've worked as a camp counselor, and volunteered for four years at a local hospital, helping out on the pediatric ward. I love to read, and I'm a natural storyteller. Some of my poems and stories have even been published.

DIALOGUING WITH WHAT YOU LOVE

Begin a written dialogue between you and what you love. Treat the dialogue as though it were a regular conversation. Take turns speaking from your voice and the imaginery voice of what you love. Continue with this dialogue until you reach some form of resolution. Begin new dialogues as needed.

The focused free-form writing helped Carla get in touch with what she might want to do, but she now felt worse. She had identified what she would love to do, but lamented that it seemed impossible for her to get there. I suggested she speak directly with the work she really wanted to do by creating a dialogue. Although hesitant at first, she began the dialogue in my office.

ME: I don't get what I'm supposed to do. How can I talk to you if I'm still figuring out who you are?

WORK I REALLY LOVE: That's true, you don't know me yet, but I know you and I know you're not happy with what you're doing.

ME: Well, life isn't always about being happy. Some things just are the way they are.

WORK I REALLY LOVE: Maybe, but are you at least willing to hear what I have to say?

I saw that Carla was off to a good start and suggested she complete the dialogue on her own for our next session. The following week she returned and shared the rest of her dialogue.

ME: Okay, I'm willing to hear what you have to say.

WORK I REALLY LOVE: Okay. First of all, what you're doing isn't all that bad. It's not like you're in prison or being treated badly. It may not be your heart's desire, but there is certainly nothing wrong with it.

ME: I know that.

WORK I REALLY LOVE: All I want to ask you to do is consider some ways you can bring me into your life. Consider options. Think about alternatives. Start planning. You don't have to quit your day job to bring more of me into your life. Begin with one small thing.

ME: What do you mean?

WORK I REALLY LOVE: For example, you can still do volunteer work at the hospital like you used to. You can make sure you get to the office on time or early so you can leave on time, or even leave early. Don't take on any extra things at work. For now it's just your job.

ME: Go on . . .

WORK I REALLY LOVE: Also, there's no reason you can't do your reading and writing in the evenings and on weekends. You just have to get better organized and schedule it. You can set up time each evening to work on your children's book. See, I think the thing is you have been making this black and white, and it's not. There are many shades of gray in between. Make me a priority. Make a place for me.

ME: Kind of like a bridge?

WORK I REALLY LOVE: Yes, exactly. You can be working with me part-time. And speaking of part-time, there may be a point

when you can develop some business on the side and
work at your current job part-time.

ME: Yes, but what about the money? How am I going to earn a
living?

WORK I REALLY LOVE: I don't have all the answers for you right now,
but I know that there are some small steps you can take
to get started moving in my direction.

Carla continued to use this technique for some time. Eventually
she went back to school to finish her degree in library science.
She transitioned out of her job and became an elementary school
librarian, where she was able to continue to write children's stories
and work with young children. What is important about Carla is that
she was able to identify what it is that she loved to do and what she
did well and then make a plan to get there.

ME AT MY BEST COLLAGE

> Create a collage illustrating you at your best, or the way you
> would like to be. Use magazines, photos, or other sources for
> pictures. Images can be real or imagined, concrete and specific,
> or any combination.

Occasionally I suggest to a client to try what I think of as a cross-
training exercise. By *cross-training* I mean using other mediums sepa-
rately or in combination with more traditional journaling. I used such
an example in Chapter 7 when I discussed Nature Walk and Write. In
that case, a nature walk was used in combination with writing.

In a Me at My Best Collage, the client is invited to use art in combination with writing. I describe the exercise to the client in the following way: Using magazines, photos, or other sources, create a collage

of you at your very best or the way you would like to be. Images can either be real, imagined, concrete and specific, playful or any combination. Add words, quotations, or whatever else inspires you.

I once explained creating a collage to a woman who had no idea what I was talking about and asked me about what type of magazines, what kind of photos, what color paper to use, and so on. There are some people who do not relate at all to this exercise; in that case, skip it and move on to something else. On the other hand, I have found many times that both clients and students love this sort of project and become quite energized by it.

I recall an occasion when a woman I had met in a class later came to see me as a client. She sat in the waiting room, holding the collage she had made in class, now framed so she could put it up on her wall. For some people, creating in a visual medium such as a collage can be very powerful. Doing collage work can be quite meditative and soothing. It's also a highly intuitive process. Perhaps when it comes to collage making, the old adage "a picture is worth a thousand words" is true.

STRENGTHS INTRODUCTION

> Take a moment to consider one of your strengths, something you know you do well. Write an introduction of yourself that illustrates this strength. If you have an opportunity to do so, share your introduction with someone else.

Psychologists Robert Diener and Ben Dean describe an exercise called a Strengths Introduction (Biswas-Diener and Dean, 2007). This is a great exercise to be used in an individual session, and it also works very well as an icebreaker for a group session. Unless you're a narcissist, this exercise is more difficult than it sounds. Clients are asked to introduce themselves via a story that illustrates their strengths.

Most people are less than comfortable bragging about themselves. For someone with low self-esteem, it can be an even bigger challenge.

Roxanne, a member of a new biweekly women's group I facilitated, was especially challenged by this exercise. She was a quiet woman and introverted in social situations. Yet I knew that she had a wicked sense of humor and could probably do stand-up comedy if she wanted. I asked all of the women to introduce themselves by writing a Strengths Introduction. The rest of the group checked in and read their introductions. Roxanne had written out a full page, but she looked to me as though she wished she could fall through a hole in the floor rather than read her introduction to the group. I gently asked her if she would like to share her Strengths Introduction.

"Not really," she said, "but thanks." A few of the women smiled. Roxanne than picked up a sheaf of paper and said quietly, "Well I have written a *few* words," letting several sheets fall from her fingers. By now the entire group was sitting with rapt attention, waiting for her to go on. She read the Strengths Introduction she had written. She told a charming and funny, although slightly self-effacing story about losing her phone. By the time she finished, the entire group was laughing.

I asked if anyone had any feedback for Roxanne. Hands shot up all over the room. One after another, the women gave her very positive feedback about her introduction and told her how much they enjoyed her sense of humor. For others in the group, but especially for Roxanne, there were two positive things to take away. First, the writing of the Strengths Introduction focuses attention on the positive qualities or traits we are likely to be aware of but tend to minimize. Second, once shared with either you, the therapist, or others in a group setting, getting direct positive feedback from the Strengths Introduction makes it difficult to ignore.

In another case, I asked another client, Al, to write a Strengths Introduction, introducing himself via a story that illustrates one of his strengths. This is what he wrote:

I played team sports throughout high school and lettered in basketball. When I was in college, I frequently found pick-up games and joined in at local playgrounds around town. I began to notice a bunch of younger kids, hanging out at one particular court. They didn't get out and play, but they watched every move. One day I went up to one of the guys and asked if he wanted to play. He hesitated for about 30 seconds, then nodded. Soon, his friends joined in. By the time I graduated from college, I had established a youth basketball league for those kids. I guess I'm pretty good at leadership and teamwork.

As I got to know him better, I learned that Al was quite modest. Even writing the foregoing Strengths Introduction had been very difficult for him. Al had done extremely well in school—he was a high achiever and an outstanding athlete. However, he had grown up with two parents who minimized his achievements, barely acknowledging his many gifts. Quite naturally, he had done the same. For many clients, the Strengths Introduction is a turning point, the first experience in viewing themselves from a completely new perspective.

CHANGE YOUR PERSPECTIVE

Select an incident from your past or a current situation that troubles you. Sit quietly and think about the incident. See it clearly in your mind's eye. Now, pretend you are a stranger or from another planet and observe the same scene. Take a few minutes and write about what you notice. How has your perspective changed?

Elaine was 35 years old, but she looked older. She had grown up in an inordinately abusive household. I noticed that as I was speaking with her, she had trouble maintaining eye contact and seemed restless and fidgety, uncomfortable in her own body. Elaine likely had very little that made her happy. But what she probably did have, I reasoned, was resilience. Even with chronic low self-esteem, she was a person who had survived.

I had skimmed Elaine's biographical statement after her first session. It had been difficult to read. I decided to use it the following way: I asked her if she would be willing to try an experiment. She nodded. I asked if she would mind taking an incident from her childhood, and although there was no need to say anything aloud, just to picture it in her mind's eye. She closed her eyes and I waited a few moments.

"Now," I began, "I would like you to pretend you are a person from another planet, and you are observing this scene." Elaine nodded. "Look carefully at the little girl and tell me what you see." She didn't respond for several minutes and I thought that perhaps she hadn't heard me. Then I noticed tears streaming down her cheeks. In a very quiet voice, she said, "She must have been terrified." And then, "Oh my God, what a brave little girl." For a moment we both sat in silence. Finally, I said, "Yes, I think she was incredibly brave. Brave, and strong, and resilient, and amazing."

I asked Elaine if she would be willing to take one such incident every day for a week and write a brief summary of what she observed about that little girl. She agreed to do so. I had no idea what to expect.

When Elaine returned the following week, she still had much sadness in her eyes, but she looked lighter, more alive. I asked her how the week had gone and what she had noticed about the little girl. She handed me her notebook. Here is part of what she had written.

- Incident one: I looked into the eyes of that little girl and my heart ached for her. She seemed wise beyond her years.

- Incident two: This time I saw not just the little girl but also an adult off in the corner. I wanted to punch his lights out for hurting this child.
- Incident three: This was weird, but when I looked at the little girl this time, I just wanted to scoop her up into my arms and take her away.

As Elaine and I talked about what this journaling experience had been like for her, she told me that as many times as she had pictured these incidents in her mind, she had always done so from the perspective of the child. She had never really thought of looking at these scenarios from the perspective of an adult. She didn't stay in therapy long, but it is my hope that her change in perspective continued.

GRATITUDE 101

Sit quietly in a place where you will not be disturbed. When you are ready, begin a list in your journal or a notebook of things that you are grateful for. It's fine if you repeat things. Keep this list handy and add to it whenever you think of another thing that you are grateful for or that makes you happy. Refer to this list often.

At a writing retreat some years ago, I was fortunate enough to be in a lovely room where I could look out and see the Pacific Ocean. For some reason, I became obsessed with the fact that a skylight in my room was locked and I was unable to find a way to open it. The next day I realized how ridiculous it was to be obsessed with what I couldn't have when I was in such a beautiful place. So I decided to offset the negative thought by starting a list of what I did have and what things in my life made me happy. Hesitant at first, I got increasingly energized as I added labyrinth walks, my grandchildren, waterfalls, and quiet streams. I continued the list for several days, challenging myself to write down 101 things for which I was grateful.

This is a simple gratitude list, yet it has a cumulative effect. The more things that are added to the list, the easier it becomes to continue to find more.

As psychotherapists, it is natural for us to focus on psychopathology. We are trained to diagnose psychological problems. However, throughout this chapter you have probably noticed an emphasis on identifying and using personal strengths as a means of raising self-esteem. This focus is purposeful, based on empirical validation (Seligman et al., 2005). It seems when we are doing what we do best, we feel better about ourselves.

Another important theme throughout this chapter is the ability to change perspective. Sometimes, just the slightest shift in perception can make a significant difference. On occasion, using the confines of my office, I ask a client to take an issue or concern and imagine placing it in the center of the room. Then, walking around together to different points on the periphery of the office, I suggest looking at the scenario again. This is a simple exercise, and like many of the journaling exercises presented here, it is a powerful step toward healing.

CHAPTER *11*

Distressed Couples and Families

*I*f you are a psychotherapist trained in couples therapy or family systems, journaling is probably not the first therapeutic intervention that comes to mind. Yet there are a surprising number of writing interventions that work quite well. Marriage Encounter is a religiously based couples' weekend workshop that has been in existence for over 60 years. One of the primary communication tools used in their workshop is a notebook in which couples write down responses to discussion questions and then trade notebooks, sharing their responses. Imago workshops, based on Harville Hendrix's book *Getting the Love You Want* (2001), uses a manual with written exercises.

In couples therapy, written assignments may serve as a way to bring the structure of the therapy session home. In this way couples can practice newly learned skills in the very real conditions of everyday life with its many distractions and interruptions, household chores, and issues with children (Epstein and Baucom, 2007). In family therapy, the use of written assignments can help strengthen problem-solving abilities and communication among family members as well as nurture attachment and help build the family structure (Rekart and Lebow, 2007).

FIRST ATTRACTION LIST

Working with your partner, each of you individually makes a list of what you were first attracted to in one another. Take your time and consider carefully. Write down at least three things. Discuss what you wrote with your partner.

By the time a couple makes the decision to make an appointment for marriage or couples counseling, with rare exception, one or both are feeling left out, uncared for, or not heard. Generally the presenting problem falls into the category of communication skills. Here are two exercises that are fairly simple, yet both have the capacity to quickly help the couple reconnect. Both bring up pleasant feelings, although these are not just feel-good exercises. The goal is to return to an earlier time in the relationship when the couple was close and more connected. If a couple is incapable or completely unwilling to do these exercises, let it go. You have a more challenging situation on your hands than communication skills.

For a First Attraction List, I like to bring the couple back to a time early on in their relationship when they first met or got together. I often use journaling exercises with couples by having them start the exercise in session and get a feel for what it entails. When it seems like they understand how to proceed, I ask them to take the exercise home and continue it there.

Kelly and Bob had been married for seven years. In that time, both had been very involved in building their careers, she as an attorney and he as a management consultant. When Kelly and Bob first met, they hit it off right away. They were not just physically attracted to one another; they also shared many of the same interests. But more important than their apparent compatibility was a deep sense of shared values. Both wanted to work hard and do well in their respective careers. Both also wanted balance. Career was important, but so was family. But somehow they hadn't gotten around to the family part yet.

Kelly and Bob agreed they would participate in the First Attraction List exercise. I handed them each a tablet of paper and a pen. "Take just a few minutes," I began, "see if you can write down three things that you recall initially attracted you to your partner. It can be a physical trait, personality, or whatever else you recall."

Bob and Kelly finished their First Attraction Lists at the same time. They smiled at one another, the first real warmth they had shown since they had come in. I asked them to read what they had written. Bob went first. He had written:

- Looked great!
- Both serious and funny
- Wants a career and family

Kelly had written:

- Wants balanced life with work and family
- Physically attractive
- Great personality

I asked what they had noticed about their lists. Bob said, "They are pretty much the same." Kelly nodded her head in agreement. For a couple with a strong connection, who nonetheless had gotten off track due to work demands or lack of spending time together, this quick exercise can begin the process of reconnection. Even in its simplicity, the First Attraction List reminds a couple of why they were drawn to each other in the first place.

I APPRECIATE YOU LIST

Working with your partner, each of you makes a list of what you appreciate about one another. Write down at least five things. What you appreciate can be large, small, or in between. When you are finished, take turns sharing one item at a time. Continue with this exercise at least once a week.

A related exercise is the I Appreciate You List. While the First Attraction List needs be done only once at the beginning of the work, as a way to reconnect with the original closeness that brought the couple together, the I Appreciate You List can be repeated, and probably should be repeated several times. Once again, this is an exercise that can be started during the session and then used as a homework assignment.

I ask a couple to write down five things they appreciate about their partners. The items on the list can be major or minor, but each item needs to be truthful and sincere. I used the I Appreciate You List with Kelly and Bob. Kelly wrote:

I appreciate:
- *Your sense of humor*
- *When you cuddle with me*
- *When you take care of paying the bills*
- *When you take care of the maintenance on my car*
- *When you start the coffee in the morning*

Bob wrote:
I appreciate:
- *How much integrity you have about your work*
- *What a great cook you are*
- *Backrubs and neck massages from you*
- *How nice you are to my parents*
- *How sweet you are if I get sick*

It can be tempting to write fewer than five things. I have found frequently that the first three items on a list such as this can come to mind fairly quickly. By adding a few additional things, more of an effort is needed and tends to bring the process to a deeper level. As with Bob and Kelly, the I Appreciate You List can become a part of the couples' ongoing practice together. I leave it to the couple to determine the frequency of and number of items (not fewer than three) on their lists. I recommend doing the exercise at least one time a week, encouraging couples to come up with new items as frequently as possible. It also seems to work best if the couple is able to write and share their lists on the same day and time each week, or pair it with another activity, such as Sunday morning before a late breakfast or a Friday evening, just before bed.

COUPLE'S JOURNAL

With your partner, select a journal both of you would be comfortable using. Decide where you will store the journal when it is not in use. (If there are others living in the household make sure the journal is kept in a private place.) With your partner, discuss the purpose of the journal. What will the journal be used for? Will there be any restrictions on language or topics for discussion?

Jeff and Alexia were both quiet people, not given to great display of emotions. Both had a tendency to shut down when worried or upset, making verbal communication very challenging. I suggested they create a Couple's Journal. Some couples are simply better able to express themselves in writing than when speaking to each other directly. There are two ways to do this. One way is to have both people keep an individual journal and then share selected passages. The second way, the one I suggest most often, is to create a Couple's Journal. This involves using a shared journal to express and share feelings back and forth. The benefit of journaling to one another is that there is time in between entries to process and think about both what was written and what the response will be. I suggest to couples that they ask questions of each other and write about individual needs, goals for themselves as a couple, and so on.

When I realized that Jeff and Alexia had a fairly good relationship but had trouble expressing their needs verbally, I suggested they start a Couple's Journal. They agreed and said they would start the journal that week. Here is a brief segment of an exchange between them.

ALEXIA: I don't exactly know how this is supposed to work, but I figure it's worth a try. Somehow it's just really hard for me to express myself when we talk, so maybe this way will work better. I want you to know that I love you very much, but lately I've been feeling invisible. It's like you are physically here, but you aren't really available.

JEFF: I'm sorry. I have just been so preoccupied with what to do about my parents. Then there's work stuff, the kids, house projects. I can't seem to find any time at all for myself, much less for the two of us together. I feel badly about it, but I don't know what to do. I think I'm just stuck.

ALEXIA: I think I understand. I feel the same way, except I don't have the added pressure of caring for my parents. I do want to help and support you, but I'm feeling so disconnected. I don't want to add more pressure, but I almost feel as though we need to have a date night or something.

JEFF: Good idea. But when?

Because of the between-session writing Alexia and Jeff did in their Couple's Journal, they were able to make especially good use of their therapy sessions. Their shared journal helped them identify issues to bring up in sessions. They arranged an ongoing weekly date night. They came in for only two more sessions.

Alexia and Jeff call about once a year for what they refer to as a "tune-up," a practice I encourage. They occasionally skip a date night but have been pretty regular most of the time. They also told me they still use their Couple's Journal, but now with less frequency; they know it's there when they need it.

Here are some tips to advise your clients who may be interested in creating a Couple's Journal:

- If possible, the couple should select the journal together.
- Find a place to keep the journal and return it after each use. If living space is shared with children, other family members, or roommates, be especially careful in storing the journal in a safe place where it can remain private for the couple.
- Either on their own or working with you, have the couple set up mutually agreed-on rules such as whether there are restrictions on language or if any topics are off-limits.
- If the couple will be using the journal without restriction and both agree anything can be talked about, help them have some type of fair fighting procedure in place.
- Use the Couple's Journal at least once a week, checking regularly so as to respond to your partner as soon as it is convenient for you.

FAMILY JOURNAL

Select a journal for use as the Family Journal. Make sure it is an appropriate size and type to accommodate all members of the family. The adults will need to decide the purpose of the journal, although it is helpful to get feedback from the children. The adults will need to decide if there are restrictions on the use of particular words or topics. Determine how the Family Journal will be monitored. Plan a family meeting to discuss use of the journal.

If you see families in your practice or clinic, you might consider introducing your clients to a Family Journal. Similar to a Couple's Journal, the Family Journal is designed for the whole family. Because there will be additional people involved with the journal, it is important to be especially clear about its use. Questions such as these will need to be addressed:

- What is the purpose of the journal?
- What do various members of the family hope to accomplish by using the journal?
- Are the rules and limitations the same for children as they are for adults?
- Are there restrictions on the use of particular words or topics?
- Who will monitor the journal?

There are a number of ways to approach these concerns. Of course you might suggest guidelines for the family or integrate a discussion among family members about how the journal will be used. This serves two purposes. First, you are helping the family make some decisions about how to use the journal. Second, you will be able to get a good deal of information about how family members interact and observe their strengths as well as where more work is required.

For example, the journal may have a singular purpose and be used to discuss an upcoming family vacation. Or the Family Journal could be a place to bring up difficult topics. Or the journal could be used as a way to draw out less verbal members of the family. There are no right or wrong ways to create a Family Journal. Instead, think of the journal as a reflection of the family dynamics. What type of parenting style is used in this family? Is there a unified parental team? Is the household child-centric? Is the family organized, chaotic, or somewhere in between? Are all members of the family treated with respect and given an opportunity to express themselves?

There can be considerable variety in a Family Journal because there is considerable variety in what constitutes a family. No longer is the traditional nuclear family of mother, father, and children in the majority. National trends indicate that in addition to nuclear families there are increasing numbers of stepfamilies, extended families with several generations living together, single-parent families, grandparent-led families, same sex–parent families, plus many different arrangements of coparenting. Use the Family Journal as a vehicle to increase connectedness and communication, adjusting its use to the particular needs of the family.

Sally and Ray had been married for a year when they came to see me. It was the second marriage for both: Sally had been widowed, and Ray had worked through a very messy divorce. They were thrilled to have found each other and were very much in love. Both had two children from their previous marriages. After they purchased a new home, things went well for a while. For a stepfamily, the first stage in coming together as a family is known as "fantasy." As the new couple and the four children settled in together, many issues surfaced. Daily bickering, confusing boundaries, how and by whom the children should be disciplined all became of major concern.

Having worked with stepfamilies for a good part of my professional career, I was well aware of the stepfamily development cycle. Patricia Papernow has defined seven predictable stages necessary for a stepfamily to become fully integrated and well functioning (Papernow, 1993). Unfortunately, the early stages can be extremely challenging. In the second and third stages (immersion and awareness), feelings of discomfort, disorientation, and irritation become apparent as the new family tries to find its footing. This is the point at which many such families give up. Statistically, well over 50 percent of stepfamilies end in divorce, most during these early stages.

The middle stages, mobilization and action, are around the corner, but getting there can be fraught with difficult emotions.

Without intervention and knowledge of the developmental process, it is difficult to know what to expect.

The Family Journal is one way to help individual family members sort through feelings. Because I strongly recommend regular and ongoing family meetings, especially during these difficult stages, the Family Journal can become a critical tool for recording issues that need to be brought to the attention of the family and discussed in a calm manner. This journal is to be shared by all family members, so the adults will need to set up clear guidelines for entries written in it. The adult couple will need to spend time privately in discussion. As much as possible, the parental team will need to work toward presenting a united front when speaking with children in the household. Here are some samples of the types of entries:

BILLY (SALLY'S NINE-YEAR-OLD SON): I really like Ray. He's nice, but he doesn't play baseball and it makes me miss my dad.

SUSIE (RAY'S 12-YEAR-OLD DAUGHTER): I don't like when Sally bosses me around. She's not my mom.

RANDY (SALLY'S 11-YEAR-OLD DAUGHTER): It seems like Ray and his kids yell a lot more than we do and I don't like it. Why do they have to yell all the time?

As in any developmental process, stages move in a natural order. The purpose of communicating through the Family Journal is to help the process move as smoothly as possible.

FAMILY COLLAGE

Another approach to improve communication in family therapy is to have each member of the family create a collage representative of either how they see their place in the family or what they would like to be different. This would be a good take-home assignment, with family members bringing collages back to the session as appropriate. Collages can be very useful, especially for those who are not particularly verbal. Young children can use crayons or marking pens to express themselves.

When introducing cross-training, such as moving from writing to art, be flexible and willing to drop an idea if the direction is not working for the family. Remember, this exercise is not about creating great art, but about the process of gaining clarity in the family system, as well as increasing communication and connectedness.

ANGRY LETTER

> Sit quietly for a few minutes and focus on your anger. Take your time. When you feel ready, begin writing an unedited letter to whoever is the object of your anger. Stay focused on your anger and write down everything you can think of that is upsetting you. Put the letter aside. Later, when you are feeling calmer, decide if there are particular actions you need to take.

Sometimes one of the healthiest responses to anger regarding relationships in families is to provide an opportunity to write a completely unedited letter. The cautionary note here is to suggest to clients that what they write should be as authentic as if they were going to send the letter. The operative phrase here is *as if*. An "as if" letter allows the writer to freely and openly express what needs to be said. Because the process of writing helps sort out feelings, an Angry Letter can go a long way. An Angry Letter is useful for any family member old enough to write.

I return to the case of Gina, introduced in Chapter 4. Gina was a woman in her mid-thirties who had married a man several years her senior. Gina was on a well-established career path before she met her husband, and although she liked children, she had no intention of having any of her own. I began to notice an interesting pattern with Gina. The pattern appeared with such regularity, I actually called it the "white carpet syndrome."

The white carpet scenario consists of a woman without children of her own who marries a man with children from a previous marriage. She is career-oriented, probably earns a good living, and has created a living space that pleases her (frequently with white carpet in the living room). She is used to being in charge of her life and has an orderly and adult lifestyle.

Up until some point she has put her career first, and when the man of her dreams comes along, she falls in love. However, what comes along with the man of her dreams is his children. This is generally not part of her dream.

Gina was the prototype for the white carpet syndrome. When she came in to see me she described myriad emotions. She was overwhelmed and frustrated. She loved her husband, but she was currently very angry with him. I suggested that she write an Angry Letter. This was a difficult assignment for Gina, and she was quite conflicted. It was hard for her to express her anger to someone she loves.

I said that I understood her conflict and agreed that it is difficult to show anger at someone you love. But feeling anger and expressing it in a safe way is different from acting it out or harming someone with it. I suggested to Gina that an Angry Letter is designed for just that purpose. In her letter she was free to express what was truly upsetting to her and discharge her anger in a sort of practice session. Once she had released her anger she would be much more able to sort out the issues and speak to her husband in a calm, reasonable, and responsible manner. Finally, I reminded her that the letter was therapeutic and not intended to be sent as written.

Clearly, Gina understood what I was telling her. Here is the letter she wrote:

Dear _____,

I'm sure you know how much I love you and how lucky I feel to have found you. <u>But</u> . . . there are some things I need to get out of my system. So, here goes.

Your children appear to be devoid of anything resembling table manners. Has no one taught them basic things like "please" and "thank you?" Do they really not understand what a serving spoon is for, or placemats, or napkins? And, has anyone ever told these children not to talk with their mouths full?

I'm fine having the kids come over and swim in the pool at my condo, but leaving damp towels strewn around, and most annoying—on my beautiful antique desk chair!

I have lived in this condo for 10 years, but in one day my living room looks like a disaster and I now have pizza crumbs and tomato sauce ground into my couch and carpet.

I finally understand why stepmothers get such a bad rap . . . I could easily become a real step-bitch.

As reluctant as Gina was to write this Angry Letter, she did a very good job of expressing herself. She stated she needed to get some things out of her system, which is exactly why an Angry Letter works. I continued to work with her intermittently over the next few months. She continued to become increasingly skilled in expressing her needs and concerns to her husband.

In my experience working with couples and families, therapeutic journaling works whether the relationship is a legal marriage, living together, involvement with a significant other, heterosexual, gay, or lesbian. What makes it work is the commitment between the adult partners in the relationship, not the particular make-up of the relationship. Like any other therapeutic intervention, clients may feel some resistance, fear, or anxiety about beginning therapy. This is normal, but too much resistance undermines the process. Remember, if a client's reluctance is so pronounced as to avoid all participation in journaling exercises, try something else. Journaling works, just not with everyone.

CHAPTER *12*

Cravings and Addictions

*E*ven after more than 30 years of clinical practice, I am still astounded by the frequency with which addiction issues show up—whether my clients' own addictions or that of their family members, friends, and associates. Statistics vary considerably; by some counts, more than 65% of American families are negatively affected by addiction or its consequences. According to the National Institute on Drug Abuse, the cost of drug addiction in the United States amounts to more than $600 billion each year in health care, subsidized treatment, prevention efforts, damages, law enforcement, and more (http://www.drugabuse.gov).

Like many disorders, addiction is a complex mix of both psychological and physiological factors. What makes the addiction and recovery field so challenging are the vast differences in treatment options. These options range from traditional twelve-step programs to cognitive-behavioral programs such as SMART Recovery. As the purpose of this book is describing how to use therapeutic journaling as an adjunct to your work with clients, fortunately I won't have to make a decision in favor of any particular treatment. Instead, I suggest a number of writing interventions that can be integrated into a variety of treatment modalities. Remember that all treatment options work for many, but nothing works for everyone all the time (Manejwala, 2013).

BREAKING THROUGH DENIAL

> Find a time and place where you can write without being disturbed. Sit for a few moments and focus on what it means to have broken through denial of your addiction. Write down your thoughts and feelings without editing. Don't worry about syntax, spelling, grammar, or punctuation. Continue writing until this process feels complete for the moment. You may return to it at any time.

Before healing of any addiction can begin, there must be an acknowledgment that the addiction exists. That means finally breaking through the denial of the addiction. Focused free-form writing is particularly helpful during this process. Here are two examples:

I'm out of control. I think I have known this for some time, but it was just too overwhelming to admit. I'm disconnected from everything and everyone I know and care about. I feel as though I have dropped into a deep, dark hole and I know of no way to escape from here.

My wife has left me. My children aren't speaking to me and I'm likely to lose my job. So this is what it means to hit bottom. How did this happen? I was always so

focused, so clear, so sure of myself, and now I see, so
proud. Well, this is where my pride has gotten me. It
couldn't happen to me—another way to say denial.

CLEANING UP

Begin to look at the various areas of your life that will need attention as you begin your process of recovery. One way to get the big picture of the effect your addiction has had on others is to create a mind map that represents the various parts of your life. Begin by writing "cleaning up" or another phrase that describes the process of beginning your recovery repair work. Circle this phrase in the middle of a blank page. Using lines and circles, attach areas of your life such as family, work, spiritual life, and finances. For each of these areas, use additional lines and circles to describe the specific impact of your addiction.

After breaking through denial in the process of recovery, the important step of Cleaning Up begins. At this point it is helpful to get a big picture of the various areas in which the addiction has affected others. Difficult as it may be, the client in recovery will need to look carefully at each specific area of impact. The use of mind maps is especially useful here, as shown in Figure 12.1.

TELLING THE WHOLE STORY

In the process of recovery, there comes a time when it's best to just tell the whole truth about a difficult situation when you hurt yourself or someone else. Whether or not you share your story with someone else, writing down all the details for yourself will help bring closure. Sit down and become quiet. Take your time and write down everything you remember.

FIGURE 12.1

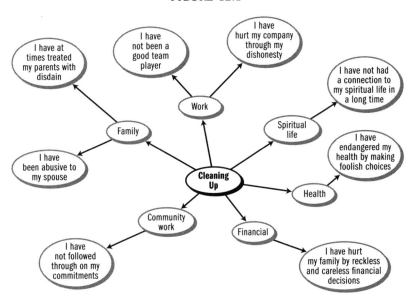

Another aspect of healing from addiction in addition to breaking through denial and recognizing the effect past actions have had on others is to tell the whole story. The complete telling of an event or story brings completion and closure. Here is an example:

I was in high school and it was senior year. We had just finished final exams and a bunch of us went out to party at the beach. We built a campfire in a pit on the sand. I still remember the smell of that fire. And I remember the beer. Beer everywhere. I remember the smell of that, too. I was completely wasted. We all were. I shouldn't have been driving, but when I got home, I banged the side of the passenger door on the garage doorframe. I told my mom, and apparently convinced her that it had happened in a parking lot. That's when I began to lie.

PLANNING FOR CHANGE

> Become quiet and let your breathing slow. Take your time and think about areas of your life you are ready to change, to make way for new behaviors. Create three columns. The first is for different areas or aspects of your life. The second is for your current behaviors in each of these aspects. The third is for the behaviors you would like to develop to replace current behaviors. You are getting ready to make the change to new behaviors.

To make changes in behavior in the process of recovery, there must be a plan in place as to what the changes will look like. For example, if blaming others has been a way of life, taking responsibility is the planned change. This exercise works well as a side-by-side comparison.

Aspects of my life	Now	Becoming
Personal responsibility	Blaming others	Taking responsibility
Honesty	Adjust the truth to fit my needs	Honest in all my dealings
Anger	Tend to act out on my anger	Owning anger and not taking it out on others
Defensiveness	Become defensive quickly	Taking ownership without defending myself

MAKING APOLOGIES

> Set aside a time and place in which you will not be interrupted. Take several minutes to become quiet and calm. When you are ready, begin to consider the people you have harmed. Create a list including each person you have harmed, how the harm was done, thoughts and feelings about the harm, the intention of the repair, and actions you will be taking to make your apology (adapted from Carnes, 2012).

One of the main tasks of recovery is to reach out and apologize (make amends) to those who have been hurt by the addict. For the person in recovery, this difficult act takes courage. To begin, the recovering addict must carefully consider each person he or she has harmed. In addition to identifying these people, it is necessary to consider how the harm was done, thoughts about the harm, feelings about the harm, intentions about the harm, and what will need to be done to make an apology (Carnes, 2012).

Here is how this exercise might look in writing:

- Harm done: I borrowed money and never paid it back.
- Thoughts: Somehow I thought this would be okay and just blew it off.
- Feelings: Ashamed.
- Intentions: Repair relationship with lender.
- Apology: Say I am sorry and pay back the money I was loaned.

PAYING ATTENTION

> Paying Attention on a regular basis requires an ongoing method of daily journaling. There are several different ways to do this. A different method can be done each day. More important than the method is the regularity of writing each day. Write a free-form entry. For about 10 minutes a day, write about whatever you notice or are aware of. Write without stopping or editing. Or, answer three questions a day such as: (1) How well did I interact with others today? (2) How well did I treat my body today? (3) What did I do to support my spiritual growth today? Or write a letter or create a dialogue with your Higher Power.

No matter how far along an addict is in the process of recovery, constant vigilance is needed to maintain abstinence. Daily journaling lends itself well as an important maintenance routine to continue for life. There are several different ways to keep a daily journal in recovery. You may choose to write every day in free-form style, jotting down whatever comes to mind for about 10 minutes or so. Or, you may choose to ask yourself some questions each day and answer them in the journal. For example, you may ask yourself: (1) How well did I interact with others today? (2) How well did I treat my body today? (3) What did I do to support my spiritual growth today?

Here is a sample of a recovery daily journal entry:

What a rich day I had today. It was Grandparents' Day at my grandson's school. It brought tears to my eyes to see how much he has grown since kindergarten. Every time I see him he uses new words, and understands so much more. Soon I won't be able to keep up with him in math! I had a melancholy moment today when I thought about what I would have missed out on if I had not become sober.

For some clients, daily journaling is a form of prayer or meditation. As part of journaling in recovery, a letter can be written to a higher power (God or the Universe). Here is a sample of a partial letter:

Dear Universe,
I am having a challenging time just now. My contract has just ended and I am now gainfully unemployed. That's where I was when I got in trouble before. I am doing fine now, but I am asking for help because I want to make sure that I stay fine. One day at a time.

Here is a brief part of a dialogue. Like the other dialogues presented throughout this book, just begin writing and let the words come.

158

ME: It's funny, when I started this program and my recovery so many years ago, I wasn't even sure I believed in you. Now look at me; I'm chatting away with you nearly every day.

HIGHER POWER: Yes, it has been quite an evolution, hasn't it?

ME: It has. I was thinking about what I wanted to discuss today and I'm having some trouble defining it.

HIGHER POWER: Let's see what you have so far and we'll go from there.

ME: Okay. There's a sense of being spacey, like I'm not quite in focus with things.

HIGHER POWER: Any idea what that might be about?

ME: I think it might have something to do with too much going on, and therefore not being able to focus on anything.

HIGHER POWER: Let's say that was so. What would you need to do to feel better?

ME: I need to spend some time alone, for one thing. I can't think straight when there's so much going on and so much inter-action with other people. And as we both know, when I am not thinking straight, I don't do well.

HIGHER POWER: We do know. All too well.

MAINTAINING MOTIVATION

Since recovery is for a lifetime, it is only normal to occasionally have flagging motivation. Once a month, respond to five questions in your recovery journal: What do I want for my future? What am I currently doing to achieve that? How do I feel about what I'm currently doing? What could I do differently to help me get what I want? How could changing what I do or getting what I want make me feel? (Adapted from Almond, 2013).

Another way to maintain sobriety on an ongoing basis is to have a motivation strategy in place. A SMART Recovery (Almond, 2013) exercise designed to build and maintain motivation to stop addictive behavior is to ask and answer these five important questions: What do I want for my future? What am I currently doing to achieve that? How do I feel about what I'm currently doing? What could I do differently to help me get what I want? How could changing what I do or getting what I want make me feel? What I notice about these questions is how similar they are to what I might ask in an actual session. The language is clear and straightforward. Here is a sample set of answers:

(1) What I want for my future is to live a clean, sober, and balanced life. (2) What I am currently doing to achieve that is I am paying attention to what I eat, working out at least four times a week, and getting enough sleep. (3) The way I currently feel about what I'm doing is that I'm just barely doing what I need to do, but not feeling overly committed to it. This concerns me because it is the way I feel when I mess up. (4) What I could do differently is really work with myself to understand about recommitting myself every day, not just when I happen to remember. (5) If I made the change of daily commitment to my health, I would feel much better and have more energy.

MANAGING URGES

Urges can come with no warning so it is important to have a plan in place. First, recognize what the urge is for (a particular food, a drink?). Write that down. What has triggered the urge? Write down the trigger. What does the urge feel like? Write this down before you act on the urge. What is your plan to deal with the urge? Write down specifically what you will do. Practice this when you are not experiencing a craving so you will have a plan in place.

160

There is no real way to get around having urges for those substances or activities from which you are abstaining. The next best thing is to have a plan in place for when urges come up, whether the substance is alcohol, drugs, food, or something else. Consider these points: What is the urge for? What has triggered this urge? What does the urge feel like? What is your plan to deal with this urge? Here is a sample:

- What is the urge for? *It's a super hot day and I really want a cold beer!*
- What has triggered this urge? *Memories of lazy summer days.*
- Describe what the urge feels like. *The urge has a sense of well, urgency, like I need to do this right now. It also feels like internal pressure, compelling, obsessive.*
- What is your plan to deal with this urge? *I will need to have an internal chat with myself that this is a momentary urge and acting on it will have way more than momentary consequences. Also, I will need to find some other behavior, like taking a walk, going for a swim, or something else physically active.*

MANAGING THOUGHTS BY CHANGING VOCABULARY

> On a new page in your recovery journal or a notebook, create two columns: "Original thought" and "Change to." In the first column list as many catastrophic phrases as you can pertaining to your recovery. In the second column across from each phrase, reframe the phrase so it reflects your thought in a more positive light. Refer back to this list as needed.

Some time ago I heard a speaker talk about using the phrase "I choose to" instead of saying "I have to," and it had a very powerful influence on me. Swapping one verb can change the entire context of this short phrase. This is a very useful skill to have in recovery. Here are some examples:

Original thought	Change to
I will die if I don't . . .	I may be uncomfortable if I don't . . .
Why is everything going wrong?	This one thing, right now, is not going well.
I'm a horrible person for doing . . .	I behaved badly when I . . .
The urge is awful.	The urge is unpleasant.

CREATING BALANCE

Begin by making a large circle to be used as a pie chart to represent life domains. Suggested categories are leisure, relationships, significant other, work, health, spirituality, education, and finances (or select categories that fit more appropriately). Divide the chart into slices to represent the current importance of various categories. Return to and adjust chart as needed to represent current emphasis or focus.

In our work as therapists, helping a client create balance is a process woven into the work throughout our time together. In recovery work, the process becomes even more critical. Discussing balance in a way that can be made visual is especially helpful. In Chapter 8, we used a pie chart to represent factors representing intentional activities that reduced depression. We visit a pie chart again, but for a different purpose here. In the sample chart shown in Figure 12.2, pieces of the pie vary in size to represent life categories.

This exercise should be repeated on occasion, perhaps three or four times a year. There is no need to judge the percentages, but use the life balance wheel as an assessment of what may be out of balance or what areas of life require more attention.

FIGURE 12.2

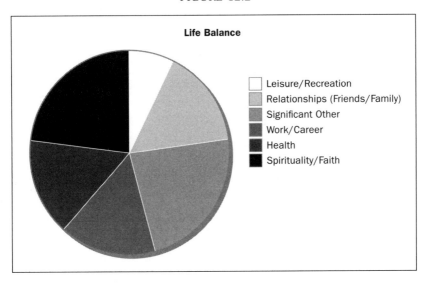

MOST GRATEFUL/LEAST GRATEFUL

You can easily set this exercise up in two columns. One column is "Most Grateful" and the other is "Least Grateful." Each day write down the things you are most grateful for and least grateful for. Refer back to this exercise frequently to work on the balance in your life.

Because balance is so important in recovery, here is another type of exercise that helps maintain balance on a day-to-day basis. I have borrowed and adapted from a wonderful children's book called *Sleeping with Bread* (Linn, Linn, & Linn, 1995), an excellent way to stay focused and in balance. Each day in your journal, respond to two questions: "For what am I most grateful?" and "For what am I least grateful?" You can do this either in a narrative format or set it up as a chart. It is a simple, yet powerful exercise. Try it! At the end of month, see what you notice. Here is a brief sample:

	Most Grateful	Least Grateful
3/1	Receiving birthday greetings	Feeling tired and achy
3/2	Saw a very heartwarming film	Feeling overwhelmed
3/3	Found a great new salad place	Missed going to the gym
3/4	Got back to the gym	Received disheartening e-mail

Doing this exercise on a regular basis is like piloting a ship. It is necessary to see both that the ship is on course, and where it has gone off course.

THE GOD BOX

Find, create, or purchase a box or container you would like to use as your God box. As you need to, write a brief note to God, your higher power, or whomever you would like to address, stating a concern you would like to let go of. Place your note in the God box and let go of the concern.

I conclude the exercises in this chapter with something called the God box. Although the origin of the practice is not clear, there is a tradition among people in recovery to keep a God box. A God box is a place to leave notes to God, your higher power, or whomever/ whatever you choose, in a symbolic gesture of letting go. I've always liked this ritual, which reminds me of the tiny box of worry dolls I keep in the drawer of my bedside table. The concept of writing something down for the purpose of letting it go is an important component of therapeutic journaling.

WHATEVER WORKS

Addiction is a complex disease that is both physiological and psychological in nature. The cycle begins with what is experienced as pain, then an attempt to relieve the pain through the use of an addictive substance or agent (or activity), followed by temporary numbness, negative consequences, and finally shame and guilt resulting in more pain (Hemfelt and Fowler, 2010). In this chapter, I have discussed a wide variety of journaling approaches that can be used with many different treatment options and approaches to addiction and recovery. Mix, match, and adapt what has been presented. Remember, there is no right or wrong treatment for addictions. The only treatment is the one that works.

CHAPTER *13*

Disordered Eating

*F*or many years the *Diagnostic and Statistical Manual of Mental Disorders* (DSM) has classified only two primary eating disorders—anorexia nervosa and bulimia nervosa. With the advent of *DSM V*, however, an important third category has been added called *binge eating disorder* (BED). Interestingly, this addition parallels what I see in my private practice: an increasing number of clients presenting with issues relating to binge or emotional eating. The diagnostic criteria defining BED includes: (1) eating much faster than normal; (2) eating large amounts of food although not physically hungry; (3) eating to the point of feeling overfull; (4) eating alone for fear of embarrassment at the amount of food being consumed; and (5) having feelings of guilt, depression, or disgust after overeating (American Psychiatric Association, 2013).

Look carefully at the criteria for this eating disorder. The bottom line is emotional eating—not for physical hunger but for underlying emotional reasons. Then, added to these underlying emotions, shame and embarrassment become part of the vicious circle. Therapeutic journaling offers several different ways to help untangle these emotions, including food diaries, giving voice to food cravings, dialoguing with feelings, and recognizing the role food plays in comforting emotions.

FOOD DIARY

One of the most effective ways to approach overeating or binge eating is to record what, when, how much, where, and most important, the feelings experienced at the time food is eaten. Many of my clients express great resistance to this process. The reasons seem obvious. If you know you need to write down everything you eat, you will think twice about what you are about to consume. The act of writing down what you have eaten forces awareness, the opposite of mindless eating.

Researcher Anne McTiernan, director of the Hutchinson Center's Prevention Center, states that the accountability factor is why keeping a food diary works. If you don't write it down, it's too easy to pretend you didn't eat that much (Kong et al., 2012). In addition, writing down everything eaten, when, and how much is tedious.

Patty had come in to see me because she had been feeling especially stressed out due to some fast approaching deadlines at work. She explained that when this happened, her usual careful way of eating went right out the window, as did her regular routine at the gym. This response to stress was the return of an old pattern and it was of concern to her. I asked Patty to begin keeping a food diary, and her response was not atypical. She responded less than enthusiastically and stared at me glumly.

"Do I have to?" she asked. "I know I sound whiny, but really I hate that."

"I know you do. It's inconvenient and bothersome. It's also effective." I think I heard her mumble, "I know," under her breath.

There are a number of different ways to create a food diary. Commercial diet programs like Weight Watchers and MyFoodDiary.com provide recording tools such as weekly paper journals and online trackers. Online trackers and smartphone applications are becoming increasingly popular due to convenience. Any small notebook would also work. The advantage of a handwritten food diary is it can be customized to individual needs. Patty kept her food diary for one week. Here is a sample that she completed representing one full day.

Date	Time	Food	Amount	Feelings	Where Consumed
3/2	7:30a	Coffee	1 Cup	Sleepy	Kitchen
3/2	8:00a	Bagel	1 large	Rushed	Car
3/2	12:30p	Caesar salad	Medium	Hungry	Desk
3/2	3:30p	Frozen yogurt	Small	Needing reward	Walking
3/2	7:30p	Hamburger	1	Tired	Restaurant w/ friend
3/2	7:30p	French fries	1 serving	Tired	Restaurant w/ friend

What makes this useful even with the few words it contains is the amount of information it provides. Patty and I were able to discuss several observations we made together:

- Out of six entries, three meals or snacks were consumed in her car, desk, or walking and not actually sitting down for a meal.
- At no point were any of her meals or snacks eaten when she was calm.
- It is difficult to determine the amount of food eaten, as there were no actual measures (how much is a small yogurt or how big is one serving of French fries?).
- How frequently are meals or snacks eaten as a reward?
- Why is she rushed or why does she need a reward?

Although the nutritional details should be discussed with a dietician, my focus with Patty was the underlying cause of her feelings and the subsequent behavior. This led to a discussion about how she responded when she was stressed and how she frequently felt like all she did was work, having no healthy alternatives for down time in her busy schedule.

GIVING CRAVINGS A VOICE

> Take a few moments to become quiet and let your breathing slow. When you are ready, close your eyes and tune into your body, feeling the sensation of the craving. Giving the sensation of your cravings a voice, begin writing. No need to overthink, just begin writing without editing.

Although she remained somewhat reluctant, Patty continued to keep her food diary with regularity. In doing so, she noticed a pattern she wanted to discuss further. She began to notice how she used food as a reward and how frequently she used sugar in particular. She also began to notice that after she ate something with sugar, she felt great right away, which was followed by what she described as a "crash" a few hours later. I suggested that she might want to do some writing about how she felt. Or, as an alternative, she could ask the food itself.

Patty's reluctance gave way as she realized she really wasn't feeling well. She also had concerns because of her family medical history with a preponderance of type 2 diabetes. This is what she wrote:

I am the voice of Patty's desire for sweet things. I know she is drawn to me. Lots of people are. Here's the problem though—many people can enjoy me and take me or leave me. But not Patty. She really likes me. It's almost beyond liking. I'm more like a "gotta have it" thing for Patty. It's like she loves me, but not in a healthy way. I think she's beginning to catch on to me. I can be deceptive, though, because I look so innocent

and attractive. What's also confusing is that I'm fre-
quently used as a reward.

Although there is some debate in the medical community, there is increasing evidence that certain foods, sugar in particular, have the same addictive properties as drugs or alcohol for some people (Avena, Rada, and Hoebel, 2007). The best way to find out if a particular food is becoming or has become addictive is to keep continuous records in a food diary.

DIALOGUING WITH OUT-OF-CONTROL

> Find a quiet place where you will not be disturbed. Take a few moments to become quiet and let your breathing slow. When you are ready, close your eyes and tune into your body, feeling the sensation of being out of control with food. Begin a written dialogue with this sensation. No need to "try" and write it. As much as possible, let the dialogue flow.

One final exercise I had Patty do was called Dialoguing with Out-of-Control. By now she knew that although the journaling exercises I suggested could seem both challenging and a bit unusual, they were effective. This was no less the case with Dialoguing with Out-of-Control. In this exercise, as I explained to Patty, the concept was to get to the core of feeling out-of-control in an effort to understand its meaning and hopefully circumvent unwanted behavior. Here is what she wrote:

ME: This is really hard; to get myself to sit down and write when all I want to do is eat something sweet. Okay. I'm going to make myself stick with this for 10 minutes. Then, if I still want to eat something, I can.

OUT-OF-CONTROL CRAVING: Wow, I must say I am impressed. You hardly ever want to actually talk to me. Mostly you just skip over that part and just respond to me without thinking. I'm almost at a loss for words here.

ME: Well, you are certainly right about that part. I know you're there, but I don't really listen to what it is you really want or need. I just seem to hear the frantic part. But given that I have agreed to talk with you for 10 minutes, I am interested in what you have to say.

OUT-OF-CONTROL CRAVING: Okay, here goes. I can be different things, at different times. Last night for example, I was a combination of fear, frustration, and overwhelm. When you eat something, especially something sweet, it calms me in a not unpleasant way. Truth be known it's not just calming, it can also be numbing. I suppose calming is okay, but numbing may not be so great.

ME: I think more to the point is this: Is there something else I can do for you or give you that might feel healthier?

OUT-OF-CONTROL CRAVING: Let me think about that. Hmmm . . . I think I was wanting some attention, some nurturing. Maybe a bubble bath, even this, a few minutes of journaling, or going to bed early. Sometimes just doing nothing is really all I need. Just being quiet and feeling whatever is going on, without having to fix it.

ME: Is there anything else you need that I can do or we can do together?

OUT-OF-CONTROL CRAVING: There is one thing. I don't know what to call it. But sometimes when I notice you really working at something, then just going on to the next thing, I feel like screaming—stop! Notice me. Give me a reward! I don't need it to be a caloric reward, although that can be quite quick and easy, but when is the last time you saw a movie? You love to watch films and you haven't been doing that. I also notice you have been enjoying some books on CD, although you only seem to do that when it's practical, like when you're driving. What about just curling up and reading a book?

Patty wrote this dialogue in less than 10 minutes. Although a single dialogue doesn't eliminate a complex issue like cravings, as Patty found, it can go a long way in beginning to clarify and sort out issues.

COMFORT FOOD STORIES

> Sit quietly and think for several minutes about the foods that comforted you as a child, adolescent, and young adult. Write down what you remember about these foods—when they were served, who served the food, what the food tasted like and smelled like, and how it made you feel. Next, write about whether you still use these particular foods for comfort in the same way.

Almost everyone I have ever talked to, even if they didn't have an eating disorder, has some memory of being comforted by food. If you are working with someone who uses food inappropriately on a regular basis, you might consider a Comfort Food Story. Begin by discussing with your client, childhood, adolescent, or young adult memories about favorite or comfort foods. Here are several partial Comfort Food Stories:

It always makes me sad when I hear all the fuss made about peanut allergies and how peanuts and peanut products aren't allowed in some schools. I grew up on peanut butter and jelly sandwiches, and to this day, I admit I still have a soft spot (so to speak) for that spongy white bread with peanut butter and jelly. I still remember my mom would cut the sandwiches in quarters when she packed my lunch.

I was sitting in my doctor's office the other day and I saw a poster about how to treat the common cold. It was a legitimate health care poster, but honestly it said to eat chicken soup as a cold remedy. It made me laugh. My grandmother was right! Her chicken soup was to die for and sometimes she added matzo balls. That soup cured way more than the common cold. She died just a few years ago and I still can't pass a good deli without thinking about her.

On Saturday nights when I was a kid my mom would make a big bowl of popcorn and my whole family would watch a movie together, while eating popcorn. I still love to eat popcorn.

I can't believe I used to eat this stuff, but as a child, a grilled cheese sandwich made with processed cheese was my idea of a great meal.

In almost every culture, food serves not just as physical sustenance but nourishment, love, and caring for and by family and friends. Draw out comfort food stories as you talk with your clients about food issues. Find out what food means beyond just something to eat.

ALTERNATIVE SOURCES OF COMFORT

If you become aware that you are using food to comfort yourself emotionally instead of feeding yourself physically, consider making a list of alternative sources of comfort. Take a few quiet moments and think about nonfood activities you might enjoy doing. Begin making a list of these activities. Refer to this list as needed and add to it as you think of new items.

Drinking hot chocolate on a cold winter day like you did as a child is perfectly fine, unless of course doing so triggers an unwanted response, such as a sugar binge or an allergic reaction. Jen came in to see me after one of her beloved cats died. She lived alone, and her pets were like children to her. She could hardly describe what had happened without bursting into tears. Her primary concern was the death of her cat, but because she knew food issues were likely to come up for her when she was experiencing an especially stressful time, she had wisely scheduled an appointment for herself.

After Jen told me about her cat, I asked her if she had been taking care of herself. "Sort of," she said at first, and then a moment later, "Well, not really. I've been going to work, of course and that distracts me, but in the evenings when I would ordinarily be going out with friends, to my yoga class, or some other activity, I just sit there. I've become a couch potato, but I can't seem to help myself." From work Jen had done with me at an earlier time, I knew that chocolate was one of the foods she had trouble with. I asked her about how she was doing with food, exercise, and sleep. She answered in reverse order. "I've been sleeping way more than usual, like half the weekend. And getting up in the mornings is really difficult, so I've been skipping the gym." She paused. "Food's not so good. While I'm staring at the TV screen I'm also eating ice cream. I know I shouldn't, but it just makes me feel better."

Almost everyone has occasional moments of eating for comfort, Jen knew she needed to make some changes in her current behavior. We brainstormed together about some alternative actions she could take. The following week, she brought in a list she had written:

Alternative (Healthier) Sources of Comfort
- Take a brief walk after dinner.
- Invite one or two people over for a quiet dinner (cat lovers), not a whole bunch of people .

- If I don't feel like cooking, pick up prepared food (that's on my food plan).
- Make a scrapbook of pictures.

WHAT AM I REALLY HUNGRY FOR?

If you find yourself eating but are not physically hungry, write down the question "What am I really hungry for?" There are two different ways you can write your response. First, using the question as a prompt, write for at least 10 minutes without stopping. Do not edit; just keep writing. Do not worry about punctuation, spelling, grammar, or syntax. Or, you can do a Quick List. Working quickly, write a list of as many responses as you can.

Although it is certainly useful to be able to find alternative sources of comfort instead of using food, it can also be useful to explore at a deeper level what true hunger lies beneath the false hunger for food. Here are two different ways to approach this search. One is focused free-form writing in which the question "What am I really hungry for?" provides the writing prompt. The second approach asks the same thing, but uses the question as a prompt for creating a Quick List.

Although I see most clients on a more regular basis (weekly or biweekly), occasionally some clients come in on an as-needed basis. Donna was a client I worked with intermittently. She was a self-proclaimed workaholic, and I wouldn't argue with this title. She would occasionally become so overwhelmed by her work that she sought less-than-healthy means to lower her anxiety and stress. One of the ways she did so was to frequent fast food drive-throughs. Donna and I discussed this pattern, but something was different from other discussions we had had in the past. She had recently had a physical and had been prescribed blood pressure medication and cholesterol medication. That got her attention. She said to me, "This has me really concerned. I'm way too young to be having physical problems like this. I need to make some changes. Big time."

I suggested that before we come up with a plan, Donna might want to see what was underneath her use of fast food when she was anxious or feeling stressed. I further suggested that she write down this question: "What am I really hungry for?" I handed her some paper, a clipboard, and a pen. "Get started now," I advised her, "and then take home what you started here and continue writing." Before she began I gave her focused free-form writing instructions: (1) write as quickly as you can, (2) write continuously, (3) don't worry about punctuation, spelling, grammar, or syntax. This is part of what Donna wrote:

> *What am I really hungry for? Huh? I never thought to ask myself that. I'm hungry for just sitting and doing nothing. I'm hungry for more sleep. I'm hungry for sleeping late on weekends. I'm hungry for a vacation. I want to go to Hawaii. I'm hungry for sitting and reading a beach novel, watching bad TV. How curious that this has absolutely nothing to do with food. None of it does. So how come I'm eating food that isn't even good?*

A second way to do this exercise is to respond to the question by creating a Quick List. That means making a list of responses as quickly as possible without editing. Here is how it might look:

What am I really hungry for?
- A well-prepared, balanced meal
- Someone to eat the well-prepared meal with
- Quiet time
- A vacation
- A great movie
- A massage
- Having my nails done

I WANT LIST

> Begin by writing down "I Want" at the top of a piece of paper or in your journal. Write down everything you can think of that you want, whether it is big, small, or in between. Use what you learn in whatever way works best—to help you focus, stop an unwanted behavior, or move closer to a goal.

An I Want List is a handy exercise to have for many different circumstances, including when you are feeling at loose ends, you find yourself doing a behavior you don't want to be doing, or you are just feeling down. It is a versatile technique, useful in many different ways. I include it here as part of the prior discussion on finding true hunger. For eating as well as other issues, knowing what you truly want is beneficial for many reasons. In the case of a binge eating disorder, as I have been discussing in this chapter, it's critical to know what the binge eating represents. Eating inappropriate amounts of food when not hungry is clearly not about the food. Binging is about not wanting to feel something, be it anger, anxiety, or even exhaustion. An I Want List can help sort out what is really wanted.

Sue had been unhappy for some time. She couldn't pinpoint the problem exactly, she just knew she wasn't happy. I said to her, "What is it that you want?" She looked at me, blinking rapidly. "What? What do you mean?"

I asked the question again. Sue responded, "You mean in my life, later today, at this minute, or what?"

I smiled. "Yes," I said, "All of the above." I then instructed her to write down the words "I Want." I suggested she write down everything she could think of, big, small, in between. This is part of Sue's Quick List:

- I want to feel better
- I want to feel happy
- I want to feel healthier

- I want to eat better
- I want to eat in a way I know is healthier
- I want a chef
- I want to exercise, but have it be something fun, not a drag
- I want to lose weight
- I want to stop feeling sluggish

Even though this exercise seems overly simple, it is still one of the most powerful of the many I use. Writing rapidly without editing is akin to stream-of-consciousness or free association.

RECOGNIZING POTENTIAL TRIGGERS

> If you are at a point in your recovery where you are ready to look at triggers that are likely to cause binges, create a list of triggers. You might want to put this in a small notebook or a piece of paper you can keep with you as a reminder. Begin your list with the most obvious triggers, such as television ads or billboards. Add to your list as you become aware of additional triggers.

In the course of treating binge eating disorder, another useful thing to know is what types of triggers will set off a binge. The answer is as varied as each individual. In Donna's case (mentioned earlier), fast food drive-throughs were an obvious trigger. For many people, TV ads of food serve as triggers. If you are working with someone who is doing well in their recovery and ready to look at potential triggers, ask him or her to begin a list of triggers. This type of exercise need not be completed in one sitting, but can remain open-ended with triggers added as they are identified.

WEIGHT TIMELINE

To gain perspective on weight gain and loss over a period of time, create a timeline by drawing a straight line across a piece of paper. Add to the timeline significant life cycle events such as births, deaths, major illness. Add to the timeline significant shifts in weight, both gains and losses.

To gain perspective on weight issues over a lifetime, a Weight Timeline is a good tool, especially for those clients who are visually oriented. A Weight Timeline is simply a straight line drawn across a piece of paper with a horizontal orientation. Along the line, have your client note significant life cycle events, such as births, deaths, major illnesses, graduations, and so on. Then, along the same line, identify major changes in weight, such as going away to college (and gaining or losing weight), getting married, being pregnant, and so on. A sample timeline is shown in Figure 13.1.

FIGURE 13.1
WEIGHT TIMELINE

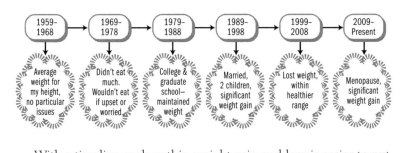

With a timeline such as this, weight gain and loss is easier to put in perspective and allows for better understanding of cause and effect of changes in weight.

For the most part, binge eating disorder has much in common with other addictions. However, what complicates eating disorders is that unlike alcohol and drugs, food is not something one can ever be completely abstinent from. As you use these exercises, please freely adapt or change what works best for the health of your client.

CHAPTER *14*

Trauma and Post-Traumatic Stress Disorder

*A*s I described in Chapter 1, the work of James Pennebaker was
critical in shifting from an intuitive understanding of the healing
power of writing to one based in scientific fact. One of the primary
aspects of the research was that inhibition of emotions makes people
physically ill. This is exactly what happens in cases of trauma. Emotions remain unprocessed. Inhibiting emotions in this way requires
physical and physiological effort. Chronic inhibition causes cumulative stress to the body and affects cognitive function as well. On
the other hand, confrontation or facing the traumatic event forces
rethinking or processing. Pennebaker states, "By talking or writing
about previously inhibited experiences, individuals translate the event
into language. Once it is language-based, people can better understand the experience and ultimately put it behind them" (Pennebaker,
1997, p. 10).

In this chapter I begin with what is known as the Pennebaker Paradigm (Baikie and Wilhelm, 2005), a clinically usable version of the writing used in the original expressive writing studies. I also discuss several additional methods for translating traumatic events into language. The goal throughout this chapter is to use writing to move through and past the trauma to healing. The exercises in this chapter are Writing a Healing Story, Dream Dialogues, Therapeutic Hate Letters, and Healing the Creative Soul.

WRITING A HEALING STORY

Over a period of several (three to five) days, write about a traumatic or emotionally significant event you have never disclosed before. Write authentically, connecting to your deepest feelings and thoughts as much as possible. Write for 20 minutes a day without stopping. Don't worry about spelling, syntax, grammar, or punctuation. Be aware that bringing up something this important may cause some mild discomfort, but it is temporary and will dissipate shortly.

In the original expressive writing studies the following guidelines were given to participating students:

- Over a four-day period, write your deepest thoughts and feelings about the most traumatic experience of your life.
- You may write about an important emotional issue that has had significant effect on you and your life.
- As much as you can, let go and explore your deepest feelings and thoughts.
- You may want to connect what you write to relationships you have with others like family or friends or to your past, present, or future. You may also want to tie your topic to who you would like to be or who you have been in the past.
- You may choose to write about only one topic during all four days or different topics on different days.

- Write continuously for the allotted time (20 minutes). Do not edit as you write, and don't worry about spelling, syntax, or grammar (Baikie and Wilhelm, 2005).

Joan came in to see me presenting with difficulties at work, including a recent reprimand from her supervisor that had left her in tears. She was having problems sleeping and felt agitated and jumpy. She knew that I frequently used writing with clients and said that she was interested in journaling. I asked Joan to write for four separate days in a row and return in a week. I also cautioned that she might experience some discomfort after the writing, but if so, it would be very short-term and would dissipate rapidly. Here is a portion of what Joan wrote:

Day 1: As a nurse I see sick people all day. It's my job— what I do for a living. So why did this particular patient get to me? He was an extremely thin, tall man, or at least he was tall the few times I had seen him walking around. Everyone looks weaker and smaller than they really are when they're lying in a hospital bed. This patient's name was Bill and something about his eyes . . . He was considerably older than me, actually he was old enough to be my father. As I nurse, I give good care, am friendly, but professional with my patients and generally get along well with the other nurses on my shift. But I found myself, if I had an extra moment or two, just "happen" to pass Bill's room. He had the kindest face I had ever seen. But now his eyes were sunken and his body ravaged by AIDS. He was a retired literature professor. Whenever he was awake I found him reading. When I came into his room, he would look up and smile, as though seeing me was the best thing that had happened to him all day. Over the course of several days, Bill shared some stories about his life, where he had studied, where he had lived, his adventures as a scholar in residence. Each evening as I did my final check on my patients before the end of my day, Bill was usually asleep. But he never failed to leave me a neatly folded note with a few lines of poetry he had written for me.

Day 4: One day as I began my shift, I walked past Bill's room to find his bed empty, and a clean set of linens tucked in crisply. It's not like I didn't know Bill was going to die, not like he wasn't close to death even when he came to the hospital. But for some reason, tears were running down my cheeks, and soon I was sobbing and gulping for air. Out of the corner of my eye I saw a tiny folded piece of paper on the floor; it must have been missed by the maintenance crew. I picked it up and of course, it was addressed to me. It was a good-bye poem Bill had written after I had left the hospital the night before.

When Joan came in the following week, she told me about what she had written, sharing some parts of the narrative. I was quite moved. She told me that she had never discussed Bill with anyone. I waited a moment for her to continue. "I think," she said, "somehow I always felt uncomfortable talking about it."

Joan had been a very young nurse when she met Bill, and she was never quite sure if her relationship with him was okay. "Was there anything unprofessional or unethical about it," I asked? "No, of course not!" Joan replied. I told her that I thought their relationship was very sweet and that while she enjoyed caring for him, he clearly had enjoyed his relationship with her.

"How lucky for you both," I concluded.

Joan had kept this bottled up inside for years, never feeling she could share it, even with a close colleague. She returned for only a few more sessions. She reported she felt calmer than she had when she first came in and her sleep was much improved. What struck me was that she had had a very significant experience, but it wasn't until she had told the story completely that she was finally able to let go of her discomfort and appreciate it.

Though this case may seem fairly straightforward as it is described, keep in mind that it is not the event itself as much as the not expressing it that caused Joan the discomfort. What triggered her agitated response in the first place was that her colleagues at the hospital wanted to give her a small party in honor of her 25th year of nursing. Joan could now enjoy the celebration.

Millie, a 65-year-old woman, was about to become a grand-mother for the first time. Instead of feeling elated at the prospect, she frequently burst into tears at the thought of it. Of course, as she explained to me, she couldn't discuss this with any of her friends, most of whom were already grandmothers. She certainly couldn't tell her daughter, the expectant mother, about it. Everyone expected her to be looking forward to the wonderful event.

Millie sat down heavily on a chair in my office. She began speaking, haltingly. "I hardly know how to say this," she began. Fresh tears welled up in her eyes. "Take a breath," I reminded her gently. She did and then continued. "When I was sixteen, I had a baby." The words hung in the air. I waited for her to continue, and then the words came out in a rush. "It was Tommy, my neighbor. We had been friends since we were little. It just kind of happened one day. Our friendship had grown up as we had grown up. We had starting 'dating,' going to the movies together, things like that. No one thought anything of it; the whole neighborhood had always seen us together. We had been practically inseparable. Sometimes Tommy would give me a kiss on the cheek, but always in a brotherly way. Then, one day he looked at me differently and he kissed me on the lips. I kissed him back. And well, you know. . . Of course, we were each others' first."

There was a lot more to Millie's story. She had become pregnant. Because she had been raised in a devout Catholic family, there had been no question that she would have her baby and then give it up for adoption. It was such a difficult session for Millie that I suggested she come back to see me early the next week. Before she left, I asked if she would be okay with writing out more of the details of what had happened and we would continue our discussion the following week. She agreed. I suggested that she not write for more than 20 minutes and that it would be a good idea to spread the writing out over several days before she was scheduled to return. Here are some of the passages that Millie wrote:

My mother and father sent me to a special "home" for girls. It wasn't as though I was treated badly there. I was well fed and cared for, but I was in anguish. My parents had forbidden me to have any contact with Tommy. Eventually, my baby was born. The nuns cautioned me to not even think about names, but I couldn't help it. In my heart, my baby boy was named Tommy. I learned later that he had been adopted by a lovely childless couple who had always wanted a little boy but could not have children of their own because of some medical reason.

Immediately after he was born, I held Tommy for only a few moments before he was swaddled and whisked away. I couldn't stop crying. For the first few years after his birth, I lit a tiny candle for Tommy on his birthday. But then, once I went off to college, I just pushed the whole thing out of mind. I married Ben, a kind, gentle man I had met at school and soon we had children of our own. I hardly ever think of Tommy, my son, or Tommy, my friend anymore. Only on occasional years have I even thought of little Tommy's birthday.

When Millie returned the following week, she was still melancholy, but much more at peace with herself. We discussed that she had never really finished mourning the loss of her son, which she was now able to do.

Five months after Millie's last visit, she sent me a beautiful picture of herself, holding her new grandson, grinning from ear to ear as she stared down at him. Millie could now be fully present and "fall in love" with her new grandson. Her healing story had been told.

Throughout this section I have alluded to this, but I want to make it more explicit: the discomfort I mention is nothing to be alarmed about, but is frequently a side effect of writing at such a deep level. It is akin to what I think of as having a good cry. You may feel sad for a short period of time—a few minutes to a few hours. Your skin may become blotchy, your eyelids are slightly swollen, and you are exhausted, spent from the emotional release. As uncomfortable as this feels physically, it is temporary and a small price to pay for the overall sense of catharsis.

DREAM DIALOGUES

If you would like to record your dreams, have paper and pen at your bedside before you go to sleep. Use an affirmation, such as "I remember my dreams with ease" if you are concerned you won't remember. As soon as you wake up, write down everything you can remember about your dream(s), even if you don't think it's important. Define the primary objects, elements, or people in the dream. Create a written dialogue between these parts.

When I greeted Marlene in the lobby, she didn't see me at first and looked almost startled when I introduced myself. As we sat down in my office, she explained the reason for her visit. She had recently been watching a film with a fairly graphic rape scene. It was unexpected, as she always made an effort to avoid films and television shows that had any violence. But this scene had caught her by surprise. She explained that since seeing the film she had been having nightmares and would frequently wake up drenched in perspiration, with her heart beating too fast.

I asked Marlene if she was able to recall any part of the nightmares she had been having. "No," she replied. "That's just the thing. I can't quite remember what happened, but I know I was terrified and felt trapped, like I couldn't escape."

I suggested several of the points I generally make about recording dreams, such as creating an intention to remember dreams before going to sleep, having paper and a pen at her bedside, and writing down everything she remembers about the dream or nightmare as soon as she wakes up (see Chapter 4 for a more complete list of dream-recording suggestions).

When Marlene returned two weeks later for her next session, she reported she had remembered a few of her dreams after trying for several nights. Here are some segments of what Marlene recorded:

I am running through a dark forest and I keep tripping over branches and tangled roots.

I can't see where I am going and there is an overwhelming sense of danger.

I keep feeling like I want to scream, but when I open my mouth to yell, nothing comes out. I don't know what happened to my voice and I am very frightened.

There is blackness all around me and I have the sensation of falling down a deep hole, or over the side of a cliff or something like that. The main feeling is of being out of control without any way to stop what is happening.

During the session I asked Marlene if she could identify the primary elements, objects, or people in this series of dreams. "There's not much to tell," she said. "Basically it's me and in each situation, I am tripping, falling, trying to yell, or in some way feeling out of control."

"Yes," I agreed. "Anything else?"

She paused. "There is something else, some nameless scary thing. It's like we're in some kind of weird dance and I'm forced to follow."

I explained the concept of projection and asked if she would be willing to have these two parts speak to one another in a written dialogue. Marlene agreed to do so. We took a few minutes of time in the session so I could make sure she understood the dialogue process. This is how she began:

ME: Who *are* you? Why are you trying to scare me? Why are you doing this?

SCARY THING: I'm surprised you don't recognize me.

ME: Who are you and why are you terrorizing me? Why am I feeling so out of control?

SCARY THING: I can't help myself. I'm out of control, too.

Marlene agreed she would continue with the dialogue on her own. Although she had originally requested appointments two weeks apart, we agreed that returning the following week rather than waiting two weeks was a good idea. As she was about to leave, I also made sure she knew to contact me if she felt she needed to, even prior to the next session.

At the next session, almost before she sat down Marlene blurted out, "there's good news and there's bad news." From the expression on her face, it didn't look like there was any good news. In the process of her dialogue, she learned that she did in fact know the Scary Thing from her dreams: an uncle she had never liked. Though Marlene couldn't put her finger on it, he had always given her the creeps.

"I don't know, he was just always weird, like he would hug me too tightly, or seem just too interested in what boyfriend I was seeing." Marlene went on to tell me that from the dreams and her dialogue with the Scary Thing, she had pieced together an incident while she was a teenager when her uncle had touched her inappropriately. Though he hadn't actually raped her, he had attempted to, and Marlene had managed to escape from him. Recently, when she had watched the rape scene in the film, the memory came back to her.

"I'm not actually sure what's the good part and what's the bad part of this memory," said Marlene. "I mean now that I know, what should I do about it?"

I had some suggestions for Marlene. One such suggestion was to write a Therapeutic Hate Letter, which might be described as an Angry Letter on steroids. In the Angry Letter, you are usually addressing someone you are temporarily angry at or perhaps have an ongoing relationship with. The Therapeutic Hate Letter is fit for perpetrators or confronting an injustice of extreme measure.

THERAPEUTIC HATE LETTER

There are times when a letter is the best way to express your hate, anger, grief, shame, or other strong emotions. Sit quietly for several moments and gather your thoughts as to what you want to say to the intended recipient. When you are ready, write down exactly what you are feeling. Do not restrict your language in any way. Do not edit or worry about spelling, grammar, syntax, or punctuation. When your letter feels complete, work with your therapist to determine the best course of action and as to whether to send it. In many cases, just having written the letter is therapeutic enough.

Here is what Marlene wrote.

Dear Uncle Ralph,
Actually I don't think you even deserve to be called
"uncle." "Slimeball" would be more like it. I always knew
you were creepy and at least now I have a better under-
standing of why. For years you came to family parties,
Thanksgiving, Christmas, birthdays. You were always so
friendly with my sisters and cousins. Now I know why.
Did you hurt them, too?

What is wrong with you, you pervert? I'm sorry Aunt
Sonia died so young, but couldn't you find other women
to be with? A consenting adult instead of your own
niece? And to think I protected you and didn't tell my
parents, because you looked at me with your pitiful
puppy dog eyes. Pitiful doesn't even begin to describe
what a sicko you really are. I hope you rot . . .

With absolutely no love, only hate,
Marlene

WRITING A PREFERRED STORY

If you have felt overpowered or physically victimized, create a story in which you have superpowers. Tell your story from the perspective of you overpowering your victimizer. Make your story as outrageous as you would like.

Although I didn't use this technique with Marlene, there is an additional exercise I sometimes use for clients dealing with trauma. This is particularly useful when a client has experienced a strong sense of being physically overpowered or victimized. I ask the client to create a new story, a preferred story with a different ending. I suggest the use of sensory details, using auditory and visual descriptions. The use of superpowers and magic are also encouraged. Here's a brief example of a preferred story:

I heard a creaking sound in the night and woke instantly. I listened intently, able to identify even the softest of sounds. I put on my hat and my glasses. I immediately became invisible and I could see perfectly in the dark. I would beat the intruder at his own game.

He moved quickly, like the cat burglar he was. But I had a few tricks of my own. I stretched a strong, thin wire between two chairs and listened. Splat! He tripped and fell flat on his face. I moved a box of toys to the top of the stairway and, still stunned from the last fall, he went head over heels down the stairs, landing in a crumpled heap. The front door opened. Two uniformed policemen walked calmly inside, cuffing the crumpled heap at the bottom of the stairs and hauling him off to jail.

HEALING THE CREATIVE SOUL

If you have lost touch with your creativity through trauma or for whatever reason, begin to set aside 10 minutes a day to spend time journaling, drawing, painting, sewing, or whatever you are creatively called to do. There are no rules, no right or wrong ways when you do creative work. Experiment; let your intuition guide you. Continue to spend a minimum of 10 minutes a day doing creative work that is meaningful for you.

I have worked with a number of clients over the years who are truly artists at heart, be it through writing, painting, music, or fabric arts. If you are not particularly drawn to these areas, it may be difficult to imagine anything traumatic related to them. Let me illustrate via a few case studies.

I have seen some of the things Natalie creates. She is a magician with fabric. She can take almost any scrap of material and make it into something else—a tiny doll for a child, a beautiful covered button, or a totally unique bookmark. She doesn't create things for a living—far from it. She is an administrative assistant and describes herself as a small cog in a very large wheel of a big business. Natalie works at her job to make a living. But her creative work makes her come alive. It wasn't always that way for her. She grew up on a farm in a small, isolated community. She was the oldest of eight children, almost a second mother to her younger siblings. Much of her life was difficult, and in her family there was very little playfulness or creativity. Her family's routine was quite clear—work hard, eat, sleep, then get up and start all over again.

Natalie managed to finish high school in three years by studying straight through the summers, while managing all the chores that were required of her at home. A few days after she graduated, she packed her bags, boarded a bus, and left. Working to put herself through school, she eventually completed her bachelor of fine arts. Unfortunately, the teaching field for her specialty was glutted by the time she graduated, and she ended up taking an administrative position just to stay afloat and pay back some of her college expenses.

When Natalie came in to see me, she explained, "I'm not unhappy. I'm just . . . " she struggled to find the words. She continued, "I just feel empty." We spoke about her day-to-day schedule and what she would need in her life to feel more fulfilled. Her homework assignment was to create something representing what was missing in her life. I sensed she needed no further instructions.

When Natalie returned two weeks later, she showed me what she had created. It was a colorful decorative pillow with designs and pictures sewn into the fabric. She had pictures of children, swirling designs, pets, crayons, and bolts of colorful fabric. I had never seen anything quite like it. As she explained each of the images, her face lit up. For her next homework assignment I said solemnly but with a smile, "Now this is going to be a challenge, but you will need to somehow find three to five hours in the next two weeks to work on one or two of these projects—something with color, fabric, or a child's art project." She smiled back and said, "Deal!"

Natalie is one of my "tune-up" clients who returns on an as-needed basis. Over the years I have learned she had begun teaching a Saturday art program for kids at the local arts center. She also frequently displays her work at local festivals. She eventually did find a position as an art teacher.

Another client, Sally, grew up in a suburban neighborhood that she described as a *Father Knows Best* kind of place. Her mother was the PTA president and her father was a member of the town council. Sally's family lived in a comfortable home, and for all intents and purposes they looked like a storybook family. Except that they weren't. Sally's father was a narcissist and undoubtedly a sociopath. She described him as handsome, charming, and charismatic. Her mother was timid, but also quite charming. She would attend PTA meetings and other events, frequently wearing long sleeves or heavy make-up around her eyes to disguise the bruises.

Her father was physically abusive only to his wife. He never hit or assaulted Sally in any physical way. But she described her father as "psychologically twisted and cruel. He didn't hit me and he wasn't sexually abusive, thank God, but he hurt me nonetheless." She described several instances in which her father almost intuitively seemed to know what she wanted and would then deliberately deny her.

Sally was a gifted musician and a budding poet. For her, practicing her instruments or writing was never a chore. Her father knew this and deliberately took away her instruments and her poetry notebooks, sometimes as punishment and sometimes for no apparent reason.

Sally learned to stop displaying any emotion at all in response to her father's behavior. In fact, after a time, she stopped displaying any emotion about anything. It was safer that way. One day she described her father in this way: "That man took away my soul."

Creativity researcher and professor Ruth Richards states that creativity can affect our health and well-being. Everyday creativity is fundamental to survival (Richards, 2007). Fortunately for Sally, reconnecting to her natural creativity was a way back to her soul.

I invited Sally to begin again what had been taken from her. I asked her if for just 10 minutes a day, she would practice her music, work on a poem, or just write in free form in a journal. She looked pained at first, and then tearful. "I don't even have any musical instruments anymore. I haven't touched a violin or flute in years. And who knows where any of my notebooks have gone."

"I'm pretty sure you can rent an instrument, and there are all kinds of places to buy notebooks," I said.

It took Sally a long time to find her way back to her music and poetry. The process was slow and difficult. "Almost," she said, "like learning how to walk again." The loss of connection to our creativity can cause pain that is real psychologically, physically, emotionally, and spiritually.

Traumas huge and menacing or traumas relatively small can affect us in unimaginable ways. Journaling provides an opportunity to organize the myriad trapped memories and details of trauma into a meaningful narrative for healing.

PART 3

JOURNALING ROADBLOCKS
AND BUILDING BLOCKS

CHAPTER *15*

Additional Guidelines for Therapists

*I*n this chapter I take the liberty of addressing some of the questions
I anticipate you might be asking. As mentioned earlier, there is a
certain amount of trial and error in the use of therapeutic journaling
with clients. Remember, there are no absolutes, only suggestions and
guidelines.

CONFIDENTIALITY

Q: How do you deal with confidentiality as it relates to journaling?

A: I treat anything related to journaling in the same way I would
   treat any other confidential material. Generally I file copies of
   whatever a client has given me in his or her chart. My office is
   located in a building made up of many small private offices. There
   is a central lobby and front desk where all visitors must check
   in. Building doors are secured after hours. My individual office is

always locked, and a key is needed to gain entry. Inside my office client charts are stored in a locked file cabinet. You may want to consider some of these precautions, the easiest of which is a locked file cabinet.

Q: Some of my clients are very concerned about confidentiality. What can I do to reassure them or make them more comfortable?

A: You may want to go through the scenario I just described, telling your client about the levels of security you have in place for their protection as well as their protection under HIPAA guidelines. You might want to explore more deeply the concerns your client has about confidentiality to see if there are therapeutic issues to address. For example, has your client had an experience when their confidentiality or privacy was breached? Did a parent or sibling inappropriately read a private journal? Even worse, did someone read a private journal belonging to your client and use this information in a harmful or ridiculing way? Those would all be issues to explore.

CONTRAINDICATIONS AND POSITIVE OUTCOMES

Q: Are there times when journaling just doesn't work?

A: Absolutely. Sometimes clients just don't like or don't want to write. Journaling can be quite helpful in moving the therapy process along, but it is not absolutely necessary.

Q: Are there specific populations who should not use journaling?

A: In my experience, clients with dyslexia or other learning disabilities are not always the best candidates. You can certainly ask, but you may not get an overly enthusiastic response. Let it go and try something else. On the other hand, occasionally clients really like to write in spite of such an obstacle. I would not use journaling with clients who have been diagnosed with a thought disorder such as schizophrenia. Clients who have had traumas specifically related to writing or who have had other performance issues can find writing difficult. You might choose to work through the trauma with your client if he or she agrees to make that issue a treatment goal.

Q: Are there specific populations who are likely to do especially well with journaling?

A: Yes. There are people who I consider to be "journal people." If journaling hadn't been invented, they would have found a way to write anyway. These are people who tend to carry around little notebooks, really like their book bags, hang out at bookstores, and are reading when you greet them in the lobby. Journal people tend to write things down without being asked to do so as an assignment. In addition to my psychotherapy practice, I also have a coaching practice in which I work with writers who are experiencing writer's block, an emotional issue related to writing, or simply want to be writing more. Inevitably they arrive at my office with a tote bag full of notebooks, journals, or books about writing they want me to know about—things I refer to affectionately as "writer stuff."

Q: Do you think some people are just naturally more drawn to writing?

A: Absolutely. Instructor and writer Linda Riebel describes this as the difference between being a *blurter* and *bleeder*. A blurter spills everything out. A bleeder writes one word at a time, each word like drawing blood (Riebel & Webel, 1998).

Q: You have mentioned that in some of the writing exercises the client may experience some temporary discomfort. That makes me nervous. Can you say more about that?

A: We have a moral, ethical, and professional obligation to do no harm. However, sometimes therapy is painful by nature. Think about going to a dentist. Sometimes you will have temporary discomfort in the process of healing. A client might become tearful, sad, or mildly depressed if they are journaling at a very deep level. However, this discomfort is temporary, lasting from a few minutes to a few hours.

JOURNALING METHODOLOGY

Q: I've heard that writing a letter to someone when you have unfinished business can be helpful, but I'm not exactly sure how this works.

A: The key to therapeutic letter writing is to write as though you are speaking directly to the recipient of the letter. Write without editing and say everything you want to say. Get it all out. Remember that this is a therapeutic exercise. Use the letter to release, clarify, and sort out feelings. Rarely should the letter be sent as is. Always take at least a day before making any decision to act on sending the letter.

Q: Is it true that writing fast can get help you get more in touch with your feelings? I don't quite understand that.

A: Yes, writing quickly, such as in free-form writing, allows you to write faster than your internal critic. If you write quickly without stopping to edit, unconscious material can surface.

Q: I understand that written dialogues are frequently used in therapeutic journaling. But how do you know what the other person in the dialogue is going to say?

A: You don't know for sure, but chances are, if you are having a dialogue with a person or entity you know, it is likely that the words will come to you once you start writing.

PRACTICAL APPLICATION

Q: I'm not clear on the logistics; does the client write during the session or as homework?

A: Both. I frequently have a client write for a few minutes during the session, just to make sure they have a feel for what they are doing. Sometimes this is not necessary. Talk with your clients to see if they understand your suggestions. Once you know your client knows how to proceed, make it a homework assignment.

Q: When do you read the client's journal? Or do you read it at all? If you don't read it, how do you know what happened?

A: I don't necessarily read the client's journal at all. Remember therapeutic journaling is about what the client learns in the process of writing, with far less emphasis on the actual content or finished product. If a client wants me to read what they have written, I do. But it is definitely not a requirement. Frequently a client summarizes what was learned from a journaling exercise and that becomes incorporated into the work of the session.

Q: Does the client read what they wrote, bring it into the session, or email it?

A: Any and all of the above. Sometimes a client will read what they wrote during the session, or a summary or specific relevant parts. Sometimes this material is sent ahead as an email. Sometimes a client prefers that I read aloud a specific part of what they wrote. It gives me an opportunity to hear it, and it gives the client an opportunity to listen to what they have written from a different perspective.

Q: Should or could the therapist ask for compensation, like a reading fee?

A: That's up to you, but I don't particularly recommend it, and here's why. If I am suggesting the client does a particular journaling assignment, that would be like any other homework. I don't charge extra to look at a client's collage, family photos, or an email. Charging extra feels like the airlines charging you for a blanket or headphones. I think it should be included because clients are already paying significant fees for treatment. If it's a financial concern for you, consider raising your fees. If a client wants me to read something, I generally skim it fairly quickly and usually it doesn't take more than a few minutes. Biographical statements take a little longer, but I make notes in the margins or highlight as I read.

RESISTANCE

Q: I'm not all that crazy about writing myself. Can I still use journaling with my clients?

A: Yes, you can still use journaling with your clients. But consider this. If, for example, you don't really believe hypnotherapy to be an effective treatment modality, even though you are trained to use it, consider the quality of the work you will be doing. Perhaps it would be useful to look at your own issues or concerns about journaling.

Q: Speaking of resistance, I'm honestly not sure if it's my client who is resistant to journaling or me. What are your thoughts?

A: As I said in the prior answer, how you feel about journaling will come across to your client even if you don't say it in words. Take a look at Chapter 16 and try some of the suggested journaling exercises yourself.

Q: What if a client is truly resistant to writing and it's not coming from me? What should I do?

A: Find out the source of the resistance. Depending on what you find, you may respond in a number of different ways. First, go back and check on the "Assessing Journaling Readiness Questionnaire" which you will find in Chapter 2 and Appendix B. The questionnaire will provide you with information about your client's background with journaling. Second, if there is trauma related to writing or other such performance issues, discuss whether your client would be willing to deal with that issue as part of their treatment. If there no apparent issues, you will want to find out if your client generally procrastinates in other areas, is fearful of trying new things, has issues with time management, and so on.

Q: What do I say to the client who is too busy to write?

A: There are times when a client is genuinely too busy to write. I found this to be especially so if a client is a single parent with young children, balancing two jobs, or is working and in school.

See if you can get agreement with your client to write 10 minutes a day for three days a week, or even five minutes if necessary.

Q: I notice you mention "don't edit, or worry about syntax, spelling, grammar, or punctuation." Why do you give these instructions?

A: Most of us grew up in a school system that corrected all of our writing mistakes, so one of the most challenging parts of working with therapeutic journaling is to get people to write without being constantly interrupted by their internal editor, correcting such things as syntax, spelling, grammar, and punctuation. For therapeutic journaling to be of the most value, it is necessary to suspend this critical feedback.

CHAPTER *16*

Helping Our Clients, Helping Ourselves

*F*or this final chapter, I invite you to a private workshop. This workshop is designed for you—to enhance your own journaling experience so you can gain the same benefits your clients will be receiving from you.

The first part of this chapter will guide you through a series of questions designed to help you determine how to best integrate therapeutic journaling into your own practice. The second part provides you with a variety of journaling exercises designed for day-to-day use in the course of your work as a therapist.

JOURNALING IN MY OWN LIFE

Decide where you will be doing your personal journaling (a notebook, online, a computer document, etc.) Take your time. When you write, don't edit. Don't worry about syntax, spelling, punctuation, or grammar. Answer the following questions. (Note: You don't have to answer all of these questions in one sitting.)

- What is my history with journaling?
- Is journaling something I have done in the past or am doing currently?
- Have I had positive experiences with journaling? Negative experiences?
- Do I have any personal traumas related to journaling?
- Do I want to pursue the use of journaling in my work with clients?
- What are my own fears and concerns about using journaling with my clients?
- What might stop me or be difficult for me in this process?

Take your time and respond to the questions about where you are with journaling in your own life. I suggest you start a journal for yourself or create a digital document for your own personal journaling:

- What is my history with journaling?
- Is journaling something I have done in the past or am doing currently?
- Have I had positive experiences with journaling? Negative experiences?
- Do I have any personal traumas related to journaling?
- Do I want to pursue the use of journaling in my work with clients?

You might also want to think about:

- What are my fears and concerns about using journaling with my clients?
- What might stop me or be difficult for me in this process?

Consider these responses from other therapists.

What is my history with journaling? "I've never been much of a journal person myself. I just don't relate to it." "I have been keeping a journal since I was 12 years old. I can't imagine not keeping a journal for myself. But journaling as part of the therapy process is kind of a new concept for me."

Is journaling something I have done in the past or am doing currently? "I have kept a journal intermittently over a period of years, but I'm not currently doing much journaling on my own." "I've actually never kept a journal except when I was feeling badly about something. But I'm seriously considering starting to journal on a regular basis."

Have I had positive experiences with journaling? Negative experiences? "Mostly my experiences with journaling have been positive. When I was young, though, I did get feedback from my father that keeping a journal was in the same category as navel gazing." "Unfortunately I haven't had the best experiences with journaling. The only time I really did much journaling was when I really depressed, so that's mostly my association now."

Do I have any personal traumas related to journaling? "Not really. In my family of origin, boundaries were generally honored. I did have an episode with writing, though when I was in the sixth grade. My teacher made fun of a paper I had written and all I remember is the whole class laughing. I wanted to drop through the floor." "I had an older brother who found my journal and then hid it from me when I was in junior high. I was mortified that he read what I had written."

Do I want to pursue the use of journaling in my work with clients? "This is certainly something I would be willing to give some thought to. I feel like I have a better understanding now of how I would go about integrating journaling into my client work." "I would give this a try, but would want to proceed with caution."

What are my fears and concerns about using journaling with my clients? "The biggest fear I have is doing something to harm a client. Also I don't feel sure of myself in introducing journaling and want some guidance or consultation." "I feel pretty confident about using journaling with my clients. Right now it's kind of like when I go to a workshop and it all sounds good, but then I get nervous when I actually have to do something new with a client."

What might stop me or be difficult for me in this process? "Just not having the experience and feeling like my awkwardness would be uncomfortable for both me and for my clients." "It's like any new thing—I will have to jump in and try it."

CLEAR YOUR HEAD FREE-FORM WRITING

If you are feeling frazzled and need to clear your head, sit down for a few minutes and close your eyes. Let your breathing slow and deepen. When you are ready, pick up your journal or put your hands on the keyboard and start writing. Write for 10 minutes without stopping. Do not edit. Don't worry about syntax, spelling, grammar, or punctuation. Write whatever comes into your head. Write down your thoughts, feelings, or what you notice around you. Just keep moving your pen or moving your fingers on the keyboard.

This is wonderful journaling exercise you can do any time. If you are feeling frazzled, short of time, and just want to clear your head, try this free-form writing exercise. Sit down and close your eyes for a few minutes. Let your breathing slow. Now pick up your pen or put your hands on the keyboard. Pay attention to your body. What do you notice? What are your thoughts? What are your feelings? Start writing and write continuously for 10 minutes. If you don't know what to say, write, "I don't know what to say." Think of this exercise as a written form of stream-of-consciousness or free association. Here are some samples.

Write for 10 minutes? Are you kidding? What am I sup-posed to write about? Okay, hold on. I'm supposed to take a deep breath. Whew! I didn't even realize I was holding my breath. I wonder how often I do that. Hold my breath, like that. Free association. Free association. Free . . . free . . . free. I'm thinking about raising my fee. I haven't raised my fee in years. I kept telling myself it was the economy, but my practice expenses are going up every year. I've got to get caught up on my filing. I hate filing. I wish charts would just organize themselves and get refiled.

I'm having a lot of trouble concentrating today. Some-times I worry if my clients knew how on the edge I am, I would have no practice. My husband and I are in the middle of a huge fight and it is making couples work rather challenging.

EMERGENCY CONSULT DIALOGUE

If you are in a bind and need to "discuss" a clinical issue and your usual resources are unavailable, you can set up an emergency consult with yourself. Create a dialogue between you and your inner consultant or inner colleague (or whatever title feels right for you). Begin a conversation with your inner adviser and let him or her be of help. Continue the dialogue back and forth as if you were having a real conversation. As soon as you are able, follow up with a proper consultation.

Imagine this scenario: You've just had an incredibly difficult morning. You have about 20 minutes to eat your lunch before a very full afternoon begins. You really need to talk to your colleague about a case, but you can't get her on the phone. You're feeling stuck and frustrated. You think to yourself, "What am I supposed to do, talk to myself?" You sit down, take out your journal or open your personal journal file on your computer. Out of desperation you start writing.

ME: I don't know what to do with this case. I really need to staff this with someone.

INNER CONSULTANT: Can I help?

ME: Who are you?

IC: I'm your inner consultant. I know you need to speak with a colleague, but for now, I'm available. What do you need?

ME: I'm having some countertransference issues with a client I need to see this afternoon. I feel like she is super-critical of me and then I practically start stuttering.

IC: I'm guessing she reminds you of . . .

ME: I have an aunt who is the same way, constantly criticizing.

IC: If you could speak to your aunt right now, what would you say to her?

ME: Well, for one thing I would tell her to leave me alone, I'm trying to work.

IC: Anything else?

ME: Yes. I would tell her I am a professional, not a child, and I need her to back off so I can be of some help to this client.

IC: Good start.

Of course I am not suggesting that you rely only on yourself for your consultation needs. However, in a pinch, creating a dialogue can be a useful way to gain perspective quickly.

INSUFFICIENT TIME TO MAKE NOTES QUICK LIST

If you are pressed for time and you know it is necessary to have accurate case notes, make notes in a Quick List format. Simply write a Quick List of what you need to remember. You don't need to use full sentences, just quickly jot down salient points. Remember to go back to the chart as soon as possible to update your notes.

No matter how well you manage your time, some days it's impossible to stay on top of things. You know you need to finish making notes in charts right after a session, but you only have a few minutes. What do you do? Using a Quick List format, you jot down the salient points like this:

- New job
- Daughter left for Europe
- Follow up on meds
- Follow up on reference to mother

This may seem obvious thing, but when you are feeling pressured you might not think of it. Jot down what you need to remember quickly and go on to your next commitment. Remember to return to the chart to update it.

LONG DAY, QUICK ESCAPE PENVISONING

> If you need a quick escape and only have a few minutes, find a comfortable chair or couch and settle in and get comfortable. Close your eyes and let yourself drift off to your own private Fantasy Island. Visualize and use your senses to be completely present in your private escape. Enjoy being present there for a few moments. Open your eyes and quickly make notes describing the scene you were visualizing. When you have finished writing, drop back in to your visualization. Move back and forth, jotting notes and visualizing.

I am a big fan of cat naps and find that just 20 minutes in the middle of the afternoon can revive me. Sometimes that isn't possible. Although it's not as good as a nap, Penvisioning can be a good substitute. Penvisioning is a process that involves visualization followed by writing and then going back and forth between these activities. Here's how it would work as a quick escape from a long day. Close your door and sit in a comfortable chair or couch. Remove glasses and shoes, or do whatever else you need to do to feel comfortable. Close your eyes and let yourself drift to your own private Fantasy Island. When you feel you are completely present there, enjoy the scene for a few moments. Open your eyes and make a few quick notes to help you remember what you have seen. Gently move back and forth between visualizing and making notes. Here's a sample visualization: "I am in Hawaii, on the north end of Kauai. There is a beach there, where the ocean meets a river. When I step into the rust-brown water, I touch the sandy bottom. The water is cool on my skin. I sink deeply into the water, feeling gentle motion. I walk further in the water out toward the ocean. A wave splashes up and I taste salt on my lips."

PROFESSIONAL ANGRY LIST

> Begin with a kernel sentence like, "I am angry with . . . ," "I am annoyed about . . . ," or even "I don't want . . ." In a Quick List format, write down as many things as you can think of that are making you feel that way. Continue with your list until you experience some relief.

If you find yourself feeling annoyed, angry, or grouchy and it is affecting your work, take a few minutes to write a Quick List. Write down everything you can think of that is bothering you. It may also be helpful to use a kernel sentence such as "I am angry about . . . ," or "I am annoyed at . . . ," or even "I don't want . . ." Continue to write until you experience some relief. Here are some examples:

- I am angry that my rent has increased.
- I am angry about the fee I receive from the managed care company.
- I am annoyed that the promised soundproofing in my office is still not done.

• I am annoyed about having to go to another staff meeting this afternoon.

QUICK ORGANIZATION MIND MAP

> If you need to organize a number of details, try creating a mind map. Put your central idea in the middle of the page. Add subpoints by attaching new circles with lines.

As you have seen throughout this book, mind maps can be used in a variety of ways. As a simple organization tool, the possibilities are endless. One big advantage of using a mind map is that unlike a written outline, additions and subpoints can be added at any time. Figure 16.1 is a sample of a partial mind map made by a therapist getting ready to go to a conference.

FIGURE 16.1

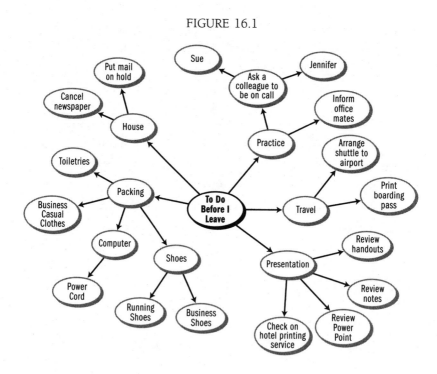

ART SELF-THERAPY (COLOR/COLLAGE/CREATE)

> Find a box or tote bag that can be stashed away or kept in the trunk of your car. Fill the container with paper, a sketch pad, marking pens, a sewing or knitting project, or whatever creative supplies you enjoy working with. When you find yourself with a break or unexpected free time, take out your art self-therapy box and create.

Over the years, when I have taught full-day workshops, one of the most interesting things I have noticed is the quiet hush that comes over the room when adults are engaged in creating. We seem to revert to a wonderful childlike place when offered paper, crayons, marking pens, and glue sticks.

Consider creating an art self-therapy box. Fill it with art supplies, a sketchbook, watercolors, magazines for collage-making, or a sewing or knitting project. Fill it with whatever you enjoy doing when you want to relax during a break. This is for you, no one else ever needs to see it. If you have a free hour or a last-minute cancellation, use some time to create.

PROFESSIONAL STEPPINGSTONES

> If you are considering a major change in your career, create a list of Steppingstones or significant events relating to your professional life. Working with one Steppingstone at a time, do some in-depth free-form writing about each time period. Use what you have learned through writing to determine your next professional steps.

This is not an exercise you want to repeat too frequently, just every few years or at times of important life transitions. Steppingstones, based on the work of Ira Progoff (1975), represent milestones or significant moments in a lifetime. For example, if you are thinking about retiring, taking an extended vacation, or considering a new part-time position instead of or in addition to your practice, Steppingstones can add an important dimension for gaining perspective. To begin, list significant events in your career, such as when you started school, earned your license to practice, took a sabbatical, and so on. As you write out your Steppingstones, you might add a few words of description. Here is an example:

- 1988: Finished master's program
- 1989: Began completing hours toward licensure
- 1990: Family crisis, everything on hold
- 1991: Continue to complete hours toward licensure
- 1992: Began studying for written exam
- 1993: Passed oral exam
- 1993: Received license!
- 1993: Set up office for private practice
- 1997: Took on first intern
- 2000: Moved to new office
- 2003: 10-year anniversary
- 2013: Consider retirement options (part-time?)

Once you have established significant milestones, you may want to do some free-form writing about the meaning of each of your milestones. Allow yourself to explore these turning points in depth.

PROFESSIONAL GRATITUDE LIST

> You can start a Professional Gratitude List any time. Or you can keep a cumulative list and refer back to it. As you become aware of those things you are grateful for in your practice or professional work, simply add them to the list. Add to your Gratitude List as frequently as possible.

Gratitude lists in general help us focus on what is good in our lives. Why not keep a Gratitude List for your professional work as well?

The list can be cumulative or you can begin a new one whenever you like. Consider this sample.

- I am grateful for my beautiful office.
- I am grateful for the clients I work with.
- I am grateful for my consultation group.
- I am grateful to be able to work in this profession.

Throughout this book, I have discussed more than 70 therapeutic journaling exercises to use with clients, as well as the exercises designed for you in this chapter. Therapeutic journaling can be a powerful adjunct to psychotherapy. Use it wisely with your clients. Take advantage of the many benefits of therapeutic journaling for yourself, as well.

Appendix A

Exercises Used in This Book

Appendix B

Worksheets and Questionnaires[1]

ASSESSING JOURNALING READINESS QUESTIONNAIRE

Have you had experience with journaling?

_____

_____

_____

_____

Are you currently keeping a journal?
If so, please describe your journaling practice.

_____

_____

_____

_____

If you have had experience with journaling, was the experience positive?
Negative? Neutral? Please describe.

_____

_____

_____

_____

[1] All appendix forms are available for download at HealingPowerofWriting.com

*Have you ever had issues or concerns about journaling or writing
in general in the past? Please describe.*

_____

_____

_____

*Have you had trauma related to writing or performance in the past?
Please describe.*

_____

_____

_____

What thoughts or feelings do you have about the usefulness of journaling?

_____

_____

_____

*What concerns do have about incorporating therapeutic
journaling into our work together?*

_____

_____

_____

_____

BIOGRAPHICAL STATEMENT QUESTIONNAIRE

Birth/Early Childhood

- Where and when were you born?
- Were there any complications at your birth?
- What do you remember or were told about your first few years of life?

Family

- Parents
  - Are your parents alive?
  - Are your parents still together?
  - If your parents are no longer living, what do you recall about their deaths?
  - What do you know about your parents' history?
  - If you had three words or brief phrases to describe your mother what would they be?
  - If you had three words or brief phrases to describe your father, what would they be?
  - What was the most important thing you remember learning from your mother?
  - What was the most important thing you remember learning from your father?
  - How would you describe the relationship between your parents?

- Siblings
  - Do you have siblings?
  - What are the ages of your siblings?
  - Are all your siblings still alive?
  - If you had siblings who are now deceased, what do you remember about their deaths?

- Dynamics
  - What was your birth order?
  - Who were you closet to in your family?
  - Who were you the least close to in your family?

School & Education

- What was the start of school like for you?
- Generally, how did you do in school?
- Do any incidents stand out about the years you were in school?

Home & Neighborhood

- Did you move around much or did you live in one home for most of your life?
- Did you grow up in a city, in the country, in a suburb?
- Describe whatever you can remember about the neighborhood you grew up in?
- What do you recall about the home(s) you lived in as a child?
- Do any incidents stand out regarding your neighborhood?

Meal Times

- Did your family eat together?
- What do you recall about meal times when you were growing up?
- What was the atmosphere like at meal times?
- Do you recall where various members of your family sat during meal times?
- What was the atmosphere like at meal times?
- What were the attitudes about eating and food in your family?

Religion & Spirituality

- Did you practice a religion growing up?
- What religion was it and what do you remember about it?

- Did your religion or spiritual practice as a child influence you as an adult?

Health & Medical

- Did you have any serious or unusual medical problems when you were younger?
- Were you ever hospitalized?
- What do you remember about your hospitalization experience?
- Did any other members of your family have any serious or unusual medical problems when you were younger?

Traumatic Events

- Was there any alcohol or substance usage in your family?
- Was there any sexual abuse in your family? If so, what do you recall?
- Do you recall any particularly traumatic events in your childhood and adolesence?

ATTENDD

To get added benefit following your therapy sessions, you can ATTENDD to what you notice by following a few simple steps. Within as little as a few minutes and sometimes for several hours or days after your session, you may begin to notice slight shifts in perceptions, new thoughts, or ideas. You may also notice changes in your moods and feelings. Try keeping your notes in one place, like a personal journal, a notebook, or a digital document. The following categories will help you keep track of what you notice.

Awareness

- Are you noticing any changes in general since you completed your session?

- What are you noticing?
- Do things seem different in any to you?

Tension/physical sensations
- Are you feeling any tension in your body? Where?
- Are you noticing any other physical sensations in your body? Where?
- Can you describe the tensions or sensations in your body?

Thoughts
- Has your thinking changed in any way?
- How specifically has your thinking changed?

Emotions
- Pay attention to your feelings. Are you feeling relieved, sad, happy, or angry? Do you feel joyous, elated, depressed, or fearful?
- Do you feel different than you felt before your session?
- How do you feel different?

Intuition
- Do you seem to be clearer intuitively?
- Does your sense of "knowing" things seem different?

Dreams
- Are you noticing your dreams?
- Note images, people, and objects in your dreams and write them down before you are fully awake.

Distractions
- Are you having any distracting thoughts?
- Is there a pattern to the distractions?

SAMPLE JOURNALING WORKSHEETS

Post-Session Keeping Track

Date of Session:_____   Session #_____

Summarize today's session:

_____

_____

_____

_____

What was the most important thing you learned?

_____

_____

_____

_____

How might this information be of help to you or influence your
behavior, thinking, or feelings?

_____

_____

_____

_____

What questions or concerns do you have that you want to discuss
at your next session?

_____

_____

_____

_____

REDUCING ANXIETY: ABCDE

Activating: What is the activating event(s) that has made you anxious, worried, or upset?

_____

_____

_____

_____

Beliefs: What beliefs do you have based on this event?

_____

_____

_____

_____

Consequences: What are the consequences of these beliefs?

_____

_____

_____

_____

Disputation: How can dispute these beliefs?

_____

_____

_____

_____

Effect: What is the effect of new disputed beliefs?

_____

_____

_____

_____

WRITE SYSTEM

The WRITE system is adapted from Borkin (2000). It can also be
used as EMDR preparation for identifying targets, and negative and
positive cognitions.

Step 1: What Are Your Current Beliefs?

Beliefs are the rules that govern you, your thinking, and your
behavior. To begin to use the WRITE system, start by making a list of
what you identify as your current beliefs. Include things your parents,
grandparents, other relatives, and caregivers told you. Include those
things you remember hearing from a teacher, minister, priest, or
rabbi. Include beliefs that came from both spoken and unspoken
rules in the home you grew up in.

Following is a list of common negative beliefs many people have
(Shapiro, 2001). Circle any that fit for you. If you are not sure, circle
it anyway.

RESPONSIBILITY/I AM SOMETHING "WRONG"

I don't deserve love
I am a bad person.
I am terrible.
I am worthless (inadequate).
I am shameful.
I am not lovable.
I am not good enough.
I deserve only bad things.
I am permanently damaged.
I am ugly (my body is hateful).
I do not deserve…
I am stupid (not smart enough).
I am insignificant (unimportant).
I am a disappointment.
I deserve to die.

I deserve to be miserable.

I am different (don't belong).

RESPONSIBILITY/I DID SOMETHING "WRONG"

I should have done something.

I did something wrong.

I should have known better.

SAFETY/VULNERABILITY

I cannot be trusted.

I cannot trust myself.

I cannot trust my judgment.

I cannot trust anyone.

I cannot protect myself.

I am in danger.

It's not okay to feel (show) my emotions.

I cannot stand up for myself.

I cannot let it out.

CONTROL/CHOICE

I am not in control.

I am powerless (helpless).

I am weak.

I cannot get what I want.

I am a failure (will fail).

I cannot succeed.

I have to be perfect (please everyone).

I cannot stand it.

I am inadequate.

I cannot trust anyone.

Below, add any other negative beliefs you are able to identify:

_____

_____

_____

Step 2: Releasing Nonworking Beliefs

The second step in the WRITE system is the willingness to release your negative beliefs. In this step, there is no real action to take, other than beginning to open to the possibility that your current beliefs were a part of your past—what was given, told or passed on to you. These beliefs may have felt valid at one time or another. Look carefully at each of your negative beliefs. Be gentle with yourself as you review them. Remember your beliefs helped you survive at some point. But it may be time to let them go.

Step 3: Identifying Memories

In the third step of the WRITE system you will have an opportunity to explore the stories and specific circumstances that created your particular beliefs. Once you know what your beliefs are (step 1) and become willing to release those that are no longer of service to you (step 2), you start step 3, which is critical to understanding more deeply the history, context, and story behind each belief. Knowing the origin of your belief may help you gain a new perspective. Here are some steps to help identify your stories:

- Select one or more of the beliefs you have listed. If you have photographs or mementos of any kind, it might be helpful to use these items as props.
- Allow some time for this process. To begin, close your eyes and let your body be in a relaxed state. When a thought or memory comes to you, jot it down quickly.
- Allow yourself to relax again. If the memories are painful or difficult, it is sometimes useful to imagine viewing them on a movie screen, removing yourself and viewing your memories from some distance. Go to your safe place if you become agitated or upset.

Make notes here:

_____

_____

_____

_____

_____

_____

Step 4: Transforming to New Beliefs

In the fourth step of the WRITE system you should now be able to transform old negative beliefs to beliefs you would prefer to have instead. The first three steps in this process were about identifying what your beliefs are and how they came to be. This step asks you to trust your ability to create new, alternative beliefs for yourself. You do not need to believe the new beliefs now. Just imagine what you would like them to be.

Go through your negative beliefs from step 1 and ask yourself, "What would I prefer to believe instead?" Following is a list of some common positive beliefs (Shapiro, 2001). Find or create a positive belief to counter each negative belief. Or add your own preferred beliefs.

RESPONSIBILITY/I AM SOMETHING "WRONG"

I deserve love; I can have love.

I am a good (loving) person.

I am fine as I am.

I am worthy; I am worthwhile.

I am honorable.

I am lovable.

I am deserving (fine/okay).

I deserve good things.

I am (can be) healthy.

I am fine (attractive/lovable).

I can have (deserve).

I am intelligent (able to learn).

I am significant (important).

I am okay just the way I am.

I deserve to live.

I deserve to be happy.

I am okay as I am.

RESPONSIBILITY/I DID SOMETHING "WRONG"

I did the best I could.

I learned (can learn) from it.

I do the best I can (I can learn).

SAFETY/VULNERABILITY

I can be trusted.

I can (learn to) trust myself.

I can trust my judgment.

I can choose whom to trust.

I can (learn to) take care of myself.

It's over; I am safe now.

I can safely feel (show) my emotions.

I can make my needs know.

I can choose to let it out.

CONTROL/CHOICE

I am now in control.

I now have choices.

I am strong.

I can get what I want.

I can succeed.

I can be myself (make mistakes).

I can handle it.

I am capable.

I can choose whom to trust.

Add any additional positive beliefs here:

_____

_____

_____

_____

_____

Step 5: Empowering New Beliefs

The final step in the WRITE system is to empower yourself with new beliefs. One way to do so is to visualize yourself as if you have already changed your behavior to reflect your new positive beliefs; write down what this would look like. You can also empower yourself with the use of eye movement desensitization and reprocessing. In this process, you will be working with your therapist using bilateral stimulation to help facilitate shifting negative beliefs and memories to new empowering beliefs.

SAMPLE PROGRESSIVE RELAXATION SCRIPT

- Allow your eyes to gently close. If you are not comfortable doing so you may choose to focus your eyes on a spot on the wall. Either way is fine.
- Take several deep, slow breaths.
- Now, begin to notice any tension in your head and scalp. There is nothing you need to do, but notice. As you take another slow, deep breath, you may feel comfortable just breathing out that tension.
- Pay attention to your face, neck, and shoulders. If you are experiencing any tension in your body, just allow yourself to breathe it out in the next exhale.
- Now pay attention to your back. Release any tension you notice in the next exhale.
- Pay attention to your chest and breath out any tension you notice in the next exhale.

- Notice your arms and hands and allow yourself to release any tension as you exhale.
- Continue paying attention to your body and breath out any tension in your buttocks and the back of your legs.
- Now notice any tension in your legs, and just breath that out in the next exhale.
- Finally, notice any tension in your ankles, feet, and toes. Just breath it out in the next exhale.
- Scan your body, and notice how it feels in this very relaxed state.

Appendix C

Basic Journaling Methods

In this appendix I describe the therapeutic journaling methods and terms I have used throughout this book.

Cross-training: Combining two or more journaling methods, such as free-form writing with collage.

Diary log: Simplest form of journaling, often considered a traditional "Dear Diary" entry, simply recording events of the day.

Dialogues: A written dialogue based on Gestalt therapy two-chair work in which one creates a written conversation between conflicted parts of the self, with others, or other entities such as work, body, or historical events.

Dream log: Dream recordings written as soon as possible after waking in the morning can provide rich unconscious material to work with.

Focused free-form: A form of free writing with no constraint on grammar, syntax, or spelling, but on a focused subject, usually used as a prompt.

Free-form: A free writing entry written with no constraint on grammar, syntax, or spelling.

Mind maps: A graphic mapping of ideas for brainstorming, planning, and organizing.

Penvisioning: A combination of visualizing and then quickly jotting notes to preserve visualization.

Quick lists: A rapid-fire method of list-making written in an unedited format to capture thoughts quickly. May be in the form of sentence completion, kernel sentences, or short phrases.

Side by side: Listing opposing concepts in columns for purposes of comparison or contrasting.

Steppingstones: A listing of chronological events representing milestones of a lifetime (adapted from Ira Progoff).

Therapeutic letters: Letters written for the purpose of expressing and clarifying feelings, very seldom actually sent.

Appendix D

Online Resources

Authentic Happiness: www.AuthenticHappiness.sas.upenn.edu

Center for Journal Therapy: www.JournalTherapy.com

Eye Movement Desensitization and Reprocessing International
Association: www.EMDRIA.org

International Association for Journal Writing: www.IAJW.org

Life Journal: www.LifeJournal.com

National Association for Poetry Therapy: www.PoetryTherapy.org

National Association of Cognitive-Behavioral Therapists:
www.NACBT.org

Radiant Recovery: www.RadiantRecovery.com

Soul Collage: www.SoulCollage.com

SMART Recovery: www.SmartRecovery.org

The Healing Power of Writing: www.HealingPowerofWriting.com

VIA Inventory of Strengths: www.VIACharacter.org

Wellness and Writing Connections:
www.WellnessandWritingConnections.com

References

Almond, R. (Ed.) (2013). *SMART recovery handbook*. Mentor, OH: SMART Recovery.

American Psychiatric Association. (2013). *Diagnostic and statistical manual of mental disorders* (5th ed.). Retrieved May 3, 2013, from doi:10.1176/appi.books.9780890423349

Avena, N. M., Rada, P., & Hoebel, B. G. (2008). Evidence for sugar addiction: Behavioral and neurochemical effects of intermittent, excessive sugar intake. *Neuroscience and Biobehavioral Reviews, 32*(1), 20–39. doi:10.1016/j.neubiorev.2007.04.019

Badal, D. W. (2006). *Treatment of depression and related moods*. Lanham, MD: Aronson.

Baikie, K. A., & Wilhelm, K. (2005). Emotional and physical health benefits of expressive writing. *Advances in Psychiatric Treatment, 11*, 338–346.

Biswas-Diener, R., & Dean, B. (2007). *Positive psychology coaching: Putting the science of happiness to work for your clients*. Hoboken, NJ: Wiley

Bolles, R. (1970). *What color is your parachute: A practical manual for job-hunters and career changers.* Emeryville, CA: Ten Speed Press.

Borkin, S. (2000). *When your heart speaks, take good notes: The healing power of writing.* Cupertino, CA: Center for Personal Growth.

Branden, N. (1995). *The six pillars of self-esteem.* New York, NY: Bantam.

Breathnach, S. B. (1995). *Simple abundance: A daybook of comfort and joy.* New York, NY: Warner Books.

Burton, A. (1965). The use of written productions in psychotherapy. In L. Pearson (Ed.), *The use of written communication in psychotherapy* (pp. 3–22). Springfield, IL: Charles C. Thomas.

Carnes, P. (2012). *A gentle path through the twelve steps.* Center City, MN: Hazelden.

Chang, L. (Ed.) (2007). *Wisdom for the soul of black folk.* Washington, DC: Gnosophia Publishers.

Cirignano, T. (2009). *The constant outsider: Memoirs of a South Boston mechanic.* Bloomington, IN: Xlibris.

Covey, S. (1989). *The seven habits of highly effective people.* New York, NY: Simon and Schuster.

Epstein, N. B., & Baucom, D. H. (2007). Couples. In N. Kazantzis & L. L'Abate (Eds.), *Handbook of homework assignments in psychotherapy: Research, practice, and prevention.* New York, NY: Springer Science + Business Media.

Goldberg, N. (2005). *Writing down the bones: Freeing the writer within* (2nd ed.). Boston, MA: Shambhala.

Halvorson, H. G. (2010). *Succeed: How we can reach our goals.* New York, NY: Hudson Street Press.

Hemfelt, R., & Fowler, R. (2010). *A companion for twelve step recovery.* Nashville, TN: Thomas Nelson.

Hendrix, H. (2001). *Getting the love you want.* New York, NY: Holt.

Kimsey-House, H., Kimsey-House, K., Sandahl, P., & Whitworth, L. (2011). *Co-active coaching: Changing business, transforming lives* (3rd ed.). Boston, MA: Nicholas Brealey.

Kong, A., Beresford, S. A. A., Alfano, C. M., Foster-Schubert, K. E., Neuhouser, M. L., Johnson, D. B., Duggan, C., Wang, C. Y., Xiao, L., Jeffrey, R.W., Bain, C. E., & McTiernan, A. (2012). Self-monitoring and eating-related behaviors are associated with 12-month weight loss in postmenopausal overweight-to-obese women. *Journal of the Academy of Nutrition & Dietetics 112*(9), 1428–1435.

Krippner, S., Bogzaran, F., & de Carvalho, A. P. (2002). *Extraordinary dreams and how to work with them*. Albany, NY: State University of New York.

Kübler-Ross, E. (1973). *On death and dying*. London, UK: Routledge.

Lepore, S. J., Greenberg, M. A., Bruno, M., & Smyth, J. M. (2002). Expressive writing and health: Self-regulation of emotion-related experience, physiology, and behavior. In S. J. Lepore & J. M. Smyth (Eds.), *The writing cure: How expressive writing promotes health and emotional well-being* (pp. 99–117). Washington, DC: American Psychological Association.

Lepore, S. J., & Smyth, J. M. (Eds.). (2002) *The writing cure: How expressive writing promotes health and emotional well-being*. Washington, DC: American Psychological Association.

Linn, D., Linn, S. F., & Linn, M. (1995). *Sleeping with bread: Holding what gives you life*. Mahwah, NJ: Paulist Press.

Lyubomirsky, S. (2008). *The how of happiness: A scientific approach to getting the life you want*. New York, NY: Penguin.

Manejwala, O. (2013). *Craving: Why we can't seem to get enough*. Center City, MN: Hazelden.

McPhee, L. (Director). (2008). *Take one step: Caring for depression* [Documentary]. USA: Public Broadcasting Service.

National Association of Cognitive-Behavioral Therapists. (2013). *History of cognitive-behavioral therapy*. Retrieved March 13, 2013 from http://nacbt.org/historyofcbt.htm

Oettingen, G., Pak, H.-J., & Schnetter, K. (2001). Self regulation of goal setting. *Journal of Personality and Social Psychology, 80*(5), 736–753. doi:1O.1037//O022-3514.80.5.736

Papernow, P. L. (1993). *Becoming a stepfamily: Patterns of development in remarried families.* San Francisco, CA: Jossey-Bass.

Pennebaker, J. W. (1997). *Opening up: The healing power of expressing emotions* (rev. ed.). New York: Guilford.

Progoff, I. (1975). *At a journal workshop: The basic text and guide for using the intensive journal.* New York, NY: Dialogue House Library.

Rekart, K. N., & Lebow, J. (2007). Families. In N. Kazantzis & L. L'Abate (Eds.), *Handbook of homework assignments in psychotherapy: Research, practice, and prevention.* New York, NY: Springer Science + Business Media.

Richards, R. (Ed.). (2007). *Everyday creativity: New views of human nature, psychological, social, and spiritual perspectives.* Washington, DC: American Psychological Association.

Riebel, L., & Webel, C. (1998). *Learning guide for critical thinking for psychology and the human sciences.* San Francisco, CA: Saybrook University.

Seligman, M. E. P., Steen, T. A., Park, N., & Peterson, C. (2005). Positive psychology progress: Empirical validation of interventions. *American Psychologist, 60*(5), 410–421.

Shapiro, F. (2001). *Eye movement desensitization and reprocessing: Basic principles, protocols, and procedures.* New York, NY: Guilford.

Sin, N. L., & Lyubomirsky, S. (2009). Enhancing well-being and alleviating depressive symptoms with positive psychology interventions: A practice-friendly meta-analysis. *Journal of Clinical Psychology: In Session 65*(5), 467–487. doi:10.1002/jclp.20593

Stone, M. (1998). Journaling with clients. *Journal of Individual Psychology, 54*(4), 535–545.

Strain, J., & Friedman, M. J. (2011). Considering adjustment disorders as stress response syndromes for DSM-5. *Depression and Anxiety, 28,* 818–823.

Thomas, O. (1966). *Transformational grammar and the teacher of English*. Lewisville, TX: Holt, Reinhart and Winston.

Tompkins, M. A. (2004). *Using homework in psychotherapy*. New York, NY: Guilford.

Welberg, L. (2012). Psychiatric disorders: Why two is better than one. *Nature Reviews Neuroscience, 13*(73). doi:10.1038/nrn3181

Zisook, S., & Shear, K. (2009). Grief and bereavement: What psychiatrists need to know. *World Psychiatry, 8*(2), 67–74.

Index

Note: Italicized page locators refer to illustrations.

Index